Graça S. Carvalho
Pedro Palhares
Fernando Azevedo
Cristina Parente
(Coord.)

Improving children's learning and well-being

Braga
Centro de Investigação em Estudos da Criança
Instituto de Educação
Universidade do Minho

We thank Ken Fitchew for the English language review.

This work was financially supported by Portuguese national funds through the FCT (Foundation for Science and Technology) within the framework of the CIEC (Research Center for Child Studies of the University of Minho) project under the reference UIDB/00317/2020.

Cofinanciado por:

UIDB/00317/2020
UIDP/00317/2020

FCT Fundação para a Ciência e a Tecnologia
MINISTÉRIO DA EDUCAÇÃO E CIÊNCIA

Título:	**Improving children's learning and well-being**
Coordenação:	Graça S. Carvalho, Pedro Palhares, Fernando Azevedo e Cristina Parente
Edição:	Centro de Investigação em Estudos da Criança, Instituto de Educação, Universidade do Minho Braga (Portugal) http://www.ciec-uminho.org/
ISBN:	978-972-8952-63-1
Data:	2020

Table of Contents

Foreword

Child Studies is an essential area of research and attention in today's society. It is in their earlier years that children start to shape their future lives. They need environmental conditions that provide them with opportunities to learn and grow up healthy so that they can develop their full potential.

It may seem that learning and well-being are separate avenues, but we firmly believe that one cannot happen without the other. Only children that have no restrictions on their ability to learn and are not immersed in distress will be able to develop harmoniously. So, both factors should not be seen independent one of the other. In fact, we prefer a holistic perspective of children.

This book brings a set of studies on children's learning, indicating the best ways to promote it. They focus on different settings: preschool, primary school and non-formal environments. Indeed, learning should not be confined to any particular setting; it may occur everywhere. It is also not confined to a specific age group; learning may occur at any age.

Studies on children's well-being and health promotion and gender equity are also a relevant part of this book. Indeed, good health is a critical condition to support all other areas of the child's development. This book originated in the Conference EDULOG 2018, which was organized by the Research Centre on Child Studies (CIEC-UM), and was held at the Institute of Education of the University of Minho. We thank the Foundation

Belmiro de Azevedo, for its sponsorship, who made the conference possible to happen.

We also have to thank all the members of the organizing committee of the conference; they were all precious help. Last but not least, we thank the authors of the texts. They were very patient and effective, so that this book can be a reality now.

Graça S. Carvalho
Pedro Palhares
Fernando Azevedo
Cristina Parente

Carvalho, G. S.; Palhares, P.; Azevedo, F.; Parente, C. (2020). Foreword. In G. S. Carvalho; P. Palhares; F. Azevedo; C. Parente (Coord.), *Improving children's learning and well-being* (pp. 5-6). Braga: Centro de Investigação em Estudos da Criança / Instituto de Educação. ISBN: 978-972-8952-63-1

Mathematics & Movement: the gallery walk strategy [1]

Isabel Vale [a], Ana Barbosa [a]

Mathematics should provide an environment that allows students to conjecture, prove, generalize, question, discuss, collaborate and communicate their way of thinking. Moreover, today we have children sitting for long periods of time in the classroom and the Gallery Walk (GW), as a learning strategy, requires students to move around the room, challenging and encouraging them to share ideas. In this context, a study was carried out with elementary pre-service teachers (for 3-12 year old pupils) with the aim of understanding the contribution of a GW for solving problems with multiple solutions by promoting productive discussions. We adopted a qualitative methodology of an exploratory nature, collecting data through observations, written productions regarding the proposed tasks, and written comments on the experience. The results allowed us to identify that the GW involved students in peer resolutions, discussions with each other and collective classroom discussions more effectively than with the traditional approach.

Introduction

The development of an effective teaching approach implies, from the teacher's perspective, the orchestration of productive discussions which involve students in meaningful learning, giving them opportunities to communicate, reason, be creative, think critically, solve problems, make decisions and make sense of mathematical ideas (NCTM, 2014). However, nowadays we

[1] Vale, I.; Barbosa, A. (2020). Mathematics & Movement: the gallery walk strategy. In G. S. Carvalho, P. Palhares, F. Azevedo, C. Parente, C. (Coord.), *Improving children's learning and well-being* (pp. 7-22). Braga: Centro de Investigação em Estudos da Criança / Instituto de Educação. ISBN: 978-972-8952-63-1

[a] School of Education Isof the Polytechnic Institute of Viana do Castelo & CIEC, Viana do Castelo, Portugal.

have students with sedentary life habits, who spend long periods of time sitting in the classroom. In this context, the gallery walk [GW] (Fosnot & Dolk, 2002) emerges as a strategy to contemplate in the classroom practice, since it meets the previously mentioned purposes. It allows students to share ideas and receive feedback about their work, engaging in rich discussions, while also enabling them to move around the classroom. In this paper we share an experience, developed with future primary education teachers, where the gallery walk was used as a teaching and learning strategy that promotes problem solving. The main purpose of this study is to understand the contribution of a gallery walk to solving problems with multiple solutions, by encouraging productive discussions. In particular, we seek to: identify the strategies used; analyse/discuss peer strategies; and characterize the reaction of the students to the GW as a teaching/learning strategy.

Types of thinking when solving tasks

Students often have preferences regarding the way they communicate and how they receive and synthesize information, which implies that the teacher must consider the existence of a diversity of types of thinking in the classroom. It has been a traditional practice in mathematics classes to have all students exposed to the same mathematical content at the same time and in the same way. However, teachers need to be aware that students may present different types of thinking (e.g. Krutetskii, 1976, Presmeg, 2014) and different preferences in relation to mathematical communication, and this may constitute a difficulty in understanding mathematical ideas, especially when the teacher uses a single way of communication.

Krutetskii (1976) distinguishes two typologies of reasoning: logical-verbal and visual-pictorial. According to this author, the balance between these two modes of thinking determines how an individual operates on mathematical ideas, which allows them to be placed in a continuum, relative to their preference in terms of thought. Several authors (e.g. Borromeo-Ferri, 2012; Krutetski, 1976; Presmeg, 2014) identify categories regarding the types of thinking used in problem solving, which are reflected in the chosen strategies. We adapted these ideas (Vale, Pimentel & Barbosa, 2018) generating the following categories: (a) Analytical (verbal) – students who prefer the use of non-visual methods, resorting to logical-verbal modes of thinking, involving algebraic, numeric and verbal representations, even with problems that could be easily solved through a visual approach; (b) Geometric (visual) – students who have a preference for visual methods, using visual-pictorial schemes, involving graphical representation (e.g. figures, diagrams, drawings), even with problems that could easily be solved by analytical means; and (c) Integrators (harmonic, mixed) – students who have no specific preference for logical-verbal or visual-pictorial thinking. These students have an integrated way of thinking because they combine analytical and visual reasoning.

The importance that geometric thinking has in mathematics is widely recognized, so it is necessary to reinforce teaching and learning with processes that allow students to develop their intuition and spatial perception (Jones, 2001). In this context, visualization is a fundamental component of mathematical reasoning (e.g. Jones, 2001; Vale, Barbosa & Pimentel, 2016), that has strong connections to geometry, and also contributes significantly to learning in other mathematical domains. Despite these positive attributes, it should be noted that visualization is not always developed and highlighted in the classroom and, moreover, there are also students who do not show a natural disposition to use it. This situation is also frequently reflected in the practice of future teachers, hence it is important to develop with them visual approaches that they can use later with their own pupils. Therefore, we argue that, for this purpose, mathematics learning should include practices that lead students to think visually and to develop this ability through tasks that require this kind of thinking. To summarize, we consider that visual solutions include the use of different visual representations (e.g. figures, drawings, diagrams, graphs) as an essential part of the solving process. In contrast, non-visual solutions do not rely on visual representations as an essential part of the process to achieve the solution, resorting to other representations, such as numerical, algebraic and verbal ones (e.g. Presmeg, 2014; Vale et al., 2016). In this study, among the tasks with multiple solutions, we focus on those that are proposed in a visual context, since, normally, they lend themselves to the use of a diversity of types of thinking, thus addressing the preferences of a greater number of students.

Movement & learning

Nowadays there is a diversity of research that highlights the existence of positive correlations between movement and learning. In this area, the field of neuroscience has been contributing significantly to the understanding of the relation between body and brain.

We can say that the body is simply an outward extension of the brain. It is through the body that we experience the world around us and the brain makes sense of these experiences. "Using the body to learn is a simple, readily available, and efficient way for students to learn and remember content" (Lengel & Kuczala, 2010, p. 8). Through movement more blood and oxygen are sent to the brain, and since we use our brains for learning, this increase in oxygen and blood flow enhances brain activity, which also can enhance learning.

Movement is an exterior stimulus of the human being. If a student is engaged in a certain task, movement indicates that his/her attention is directed toward what is being learned. When attention is purely or strictly mental (interior) the activity becomes very difficult to sustain, because the nerve and muscle systems are inactive (Shoval, 2011). If we are passive learners, then we are more likely to ignore the on-going learning process even though this may be unintentional (minds tend to wander). On the other hand, by incorporating movement activities, the learner is essentially forced to engage in the learning process, unless he/she chooses not to, making engagement observable (Shoval, 2011). As stated by Gardner (1999), who advocates for action and activity, "the brain learns best and retains most when the organism is actively involved in exploring physical sites and materials and asking questions to which it actually craves answers. Merely passive learners tend to attenuate and have little lasting impact" (p. 82).

According to Hannaford (2005), thinking and learning 'are not just in the head'; on the contrary, the body plays a decisive role in the entire intellectual process, from the first to the last years of our lives. Intelligence, which is usually regarded as a purely analytical ability, measured and assessed in terms of IQ, depends more on the body than we usually realize. Students who move in the classroom can learn, regardless of their activity, more effectively than those in typically sedentary classrooms.

Many of the mathematics failures have their origin in the emotional environment that is created, which might seriously compromise the expectations and initial motivations of the students (e.g. Hannula, 2001). In a mathematics class, in addition to the intellectual engagement, it is also necessary to consider the social and physical engagement, in order to commit students to the learning process (e.g. Prince, 2004). The focus should be entirely on the student and the activity he/she is engaged in, in contrast to a more traditional approach, in which the student passively accesses information transmitted by the teacher, a vision still adopted in many classrooms of different grade levels around the world.

From an active learning perspective, students do not learn much from sitting in class listening to the teacher, memorizing procedures or giving mechanized answers. Physical movement and emotions are central for an effective learning throughout life. The sensorimotor system relates movement, emotion and cognition, producing rich communication, which is the basis of learning (e.g. Hannaford, 2005). Beyond movement, manipulation and experimentation, students should be able to talk about what they are learning, write about it, relate new learning to previous experiences, and apply it on a daily basis (Vale & Barbosa, 2018).

Active learning strategies in the mathematics classroom

We should prioritize methodologies that require students' intellectual engagement in the construction of new knowledge, highlighting the importance of problem solving tasks and the activity that emerges from questioning. In the context of active learning, in parallel with the strategies of a cognitive nature, those that derive from social and physical activities are also important.

Active learning is generally defined as an instructional method involving students in the learning process (Prince, 2004). It requires them to develop meaningful activities and think about what they are doing. Examples of active learning strategies include problem solving tasks that go beyond the application of routine procedures, so that students have to explain and justify their reasoning. Considering that students' intellectual engagement may not be enough, it is important to shed light on the role of discourse in mathematical communication. Here the main concern is the students' engagement in an active socially mediated learning and the consideration of social interactions as one of the good practices to be emphasized in the mathematics classroom (NCTM, 2014).

As discussed in the previous section, there is yet another factor to add to this discussion, namely movement. Students, especially at younger ages, need to be physically active in the classroom. This is explained not only because, in more traditional approaches, students have long periods of inactivity and need something different to help them retain their attention, but also for physiological reasons. This need for movement can be solved by using active strategies. To address this issue, and among other examples, we can include the use of manipulative materials, the construction of models or the development of more practical projects. Analysing the previously mentioned dimensions we can certainly understand their importance from an individual perspective but, above all, as inevitably involving interactions with others. So, we may assume that learning emerges from experiences and interactions between the intellectual, social and physical dimensions (e.g. Nesin, 2012, Edwards, Kemp & Page, 2014) (Figure 1).

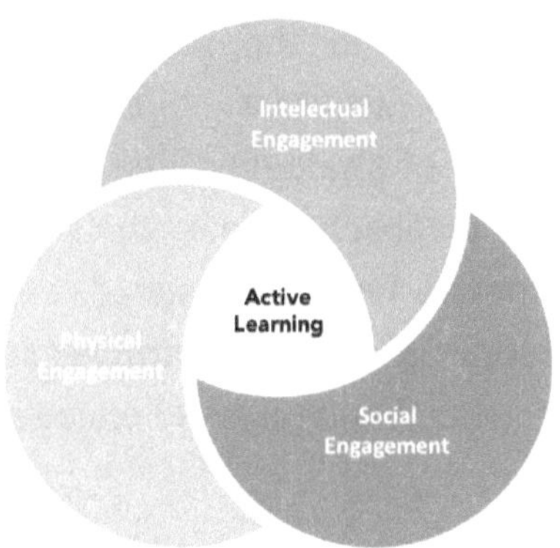

Figure 1. *Dimensions of active learning*

The GW as an active learning strategy for problem solving

Based on the principles underlying active learning, we propose the use of the GW teaching and learning strategy, adapted from Fosnot and Dolk (2002). This allows students to solve a proposed task, collaboratively, in small groups, and gives them the opportunity to present their solution through a poster that will be fixed around the classroom, in a similar manner to that used by the artists when they show their works in a gallery.

Finally, a collective discussion is held, during which each group re-displays their poster and clarifies aspects of their work. The dynamics of a GW takes students out of their seats and actively engages them with the mathematical ideas of their colleagues (e.g. Fosnot & Dolk, 2002; Vale & Barbosa, 2018). For many students, movement can help increase motivation and engagement in the classroom activity. The gallery walk also provides the opportunity for students to make contact with different ideas and/or solutions, getting written and oral feedback, which can improve their learning (OME, 2010).

Thus, the GW favours discussion, critical thinking, communication, collaborative learning, and fundamental skills that students must develop and that can be especially attractive to the more kinesthetic students. Through this dynamic, students acquire new knowledge and/or make the knowledge that is being worked more robust, and in the particular case of problem solving, by contacting different approaches/solutions, they increase their repertoire of strategies. The GW is also a way for students to receive feedback about their work in a "non-threatening" environment. For all the stated reasons, this strategy falls within the scope of active learning since it promotes students' intellectual, social and physical engagement.

Methodology

In this study, we sought to identify the strategies used by students when solving problems with multiple solutions using a GW, as well as to characterize their reaction during their engagement using this strategy. The teaching experience we describe in this paper involved the participation of 14 students undertaking a teacher training course for primary education, who attended a curricular unit of Didactics of Mathematics. In this context, a GW was implemented as a teaching and learning strategy to solve problems involving different contents (e.g. geometry, fractions). This dynamic was chosen in order to counter the perspective of mathematics as a subject that should be taught using more traditional methods as opposed to a more active approach. We adopted a qualitative methodology, of an exploratory nature, and data was collected in a holistic, descriptive and interpretive manner, including classroom observations, written productions of the proposed tasks, and a written report where the future teachers commented on their GW experience.

The GW used in this study consisted of the following steps: 1) *Task resolution* - the students solved the proposed problems in groups of 2/3; 2) *Construction of posters* – students discussed the solutions among themselves as well as how to present their proposed solution in the poster; 3) *Presentation and Observation of the posters* – after the posters of each group were displayed on the classroom walls, each student went through the room, observing the solutions presented in the posters; 4) *Elaboration of comments* - walking through the gallery, the students wrote their personal comments, doubts, questions,..., in post-its that they placed on the different posters. It should be noted that in steps 3 and 4, while students discussed peer solutions, the teacher circulated around the classroom, analysing students' observations and discussions, and attempting to clarify issues raised by the students; 5) *Group discussion* – after this round, each group collected their own poster, to analyse the content of the comments in the post-its, writing a small report; 6) *Collective discussion* - with all posters displayed once again on the classroom wall, the groups presented their solutions orally and responded to the previously made comments. This step constituted an opportunity for the teacher to highlight some of the ideas to be included in the discussion and to clarify doubts and/or mistakes, facilitating also the elaboration of a final synthesis of the fundamental knowledge that emerged from the experience (Vale & Barbosa, 2018).

Students' performance and reactions during the GW

In this paper, we chose to describe the students' performance and reactions to one of the problems proposed during this experience, solved in a GW dynamic (Figure 2).

<table>
<tr>
<td>The figure represents a square with 4 cm^2 of area, where P and Q are midpoints of two opposite sides.
Given the conditions of the figure, what is the area of the shaded part?</td>
<td>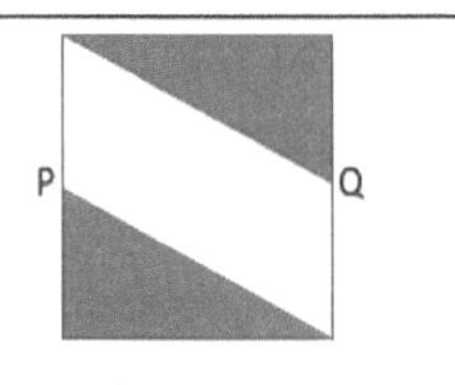</td>
</tr>
</table>

Figure 2. *The shaded square problem*

During the classes, several tasks were proposed for the students to solve in small groups. They began by solving each of the problems individually and, when they reached a solution or had doubts about the approach, they engaged in small group discussions about possible strategies to arrive at the solution, trying to identify which could be the most effective and interesting. The groups came up with solutions involving different items of mathematical knowledge and then they had to focus on seeking a solution that was appropriate for the grade level of their future pupils. The fact that they worked collaboratively facilitated the exchange of ideas and decision-making, in particular on the most effective strategy, with some groups presenting more than one solution.

After they concluded the tasks they began to decide, in each group, the best way to structure the poster with the different solutions. They made decisions about the most appropriate representations and how to write the text, among other aspects. There was some concern on the part of the students about the content of the poster and if it would be clear to those who consulted it, acknowledging the relevance of written communication in mathematics.

Once constructed, the posters were displayed around the classroom, similar to what happens in an art gallery. Each student went through the space freely, carefully observing the contents of the various posters. Individually they made comments they considered relevant and also raised questions and doubts, resulting from the analysis of posters. This feedback was written in anonymous post-its that were associated with the observed posters.

This step was followed by an analysis of the comments and questions associated with each poster. Each group collected their poster, with its post-its, and read the feedback given by their colleagues. They discussed the pertinence of the comments among themselves, the aspects they could improve in their work, how to refine the explanation of their reasoning and, in some cases, they identified errors that had gone unnoticed. Peer feedback was a positive contribution to promote reflection about the work developed.

Finally, after each group had analysed the comments and questions posed and decided if they wanted to clarify certain aspects of the poster or rectify some step, the collective discussion began. The posters were displayed in a central place in the classroom, in this case the blackboard, so that they were visible to the whole class. Figure 3 illustrates the different phases of the GW previously described. Each group had the opportunity to sum up their work, explaining the impact of their colleagues' feedback, clarifying some aspects that were not so clear and correcting some errors. This discussion was mediated by the teacher of the curricular unit who, in addition to what had already been mentioned, was also careful to focus on the diversity of strategies used. Although in this step the role of the teacher was more interventional, in the previous phases the teacher supervised all the work and the engagement of the students, supporting them whenever requested.

Figure 3. *Students executing the different steps of the GW*

Analysing the solutions to the proposed tasks, it can be said that there were no noteworthy difficulties on the part of the students. They used different approaches: only visual, only analytical, or visual solutions complemented with analytical ones. Most of the groups presented analytical solutions using the formula to find the area of the square and the area of the triangle. They chose more traditional approaches, with which they felt more comfortable, as shown in figure 4.

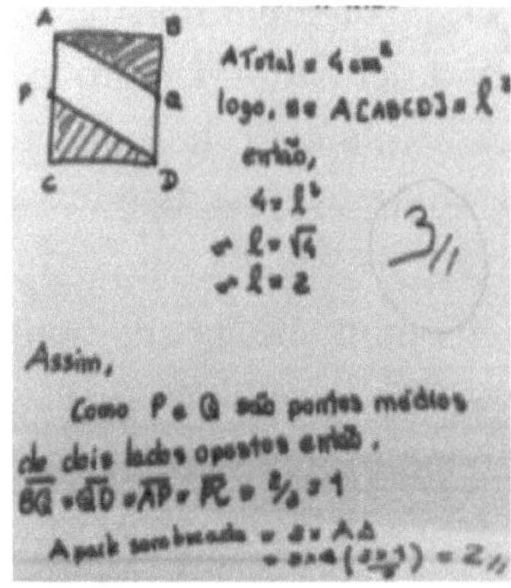

Figure 4. *Analytical solution*

However, one of the groups presented a solution that we consider of a visual nature, using the idea of part-whole (Figure 5). This solution was surprising to the rest of the students who, after analysing this approach, found it simpler and more elegant.

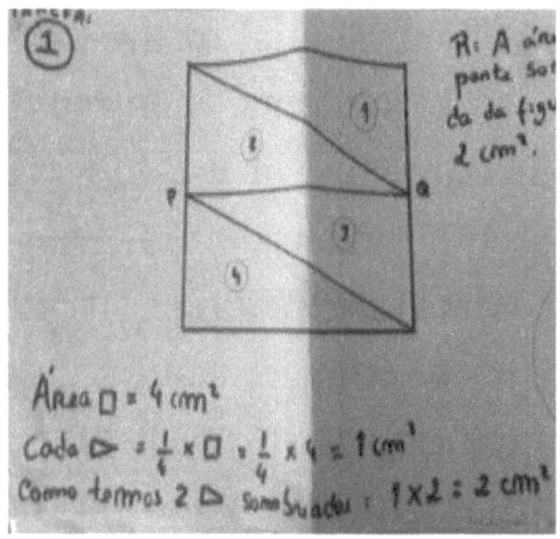

Figure 5. *Visual solution*

In the step of the collective discussion associated with the gallery walk, the opportunity arose to analyse in more detail each of the solutions presented by the different groups, answering any queries that were raised, and contrasting different ideas.

Some concluding remarks

This didactical experience made it possible not only to identify the solution strategies used by the students, but also to verify the potential of the gallery walk as a more effective way of teaching mathematics, serving as a reference for these future teachers.

The strategies used by the students, although involving the use of routine formulae and procedures, also evidenced visual solutions. We can say that the type of thinking used by the students was mainly analytical or integrated.

The gallery walk, as a teaching and learning strategy, engaged students with their peers' solutions, both when they placed their post-its with comments and in the discussions with each other, allowing them to increase their repertoire of strategies in a more effective way than in traditional discussions. Students reacted positively to the GW by expressing interest, showing motivation and recognising its importance in mathematical learning at any level. They valued this strategy for the opportunity it provided to be more engaged in a mathematical activity and discussed the potential of the use of the gallery walk in classes with their future students. Many of them manifested the will to implement this strategy in the following semester in the classes that they would undertake in their internship in the context of primary education practice. It was also possible to perceive different types of engagement by these students, such as intellectual engagement (in solving tasks), social engagement (in small and large group interactions) and physical engagement (in the free movement in the classroom). These evidences confirm the potential of the gallery walk as an active learning strategy (e.g. Fosnot & Dolk, 2002; Prince, 2004; Vale & Barbosa, 2018).

References

Borromeo Ferri, R. (2015). *Mathematical Thinking styles and their influence on teaching and learning mathematics.* Paper presented at the 12th International Congress on Mathematical Education, Seoul, Korea. Retrieved on March, 5, 2017 from http://www.icme12.org/upload/submission/1905_F.pdf

Edwards, S., Kemp, A., & Page, C. (2014). The middle school philosophy: Do we practice what we preach or do we preach something different? *Current Issues in Middle Level Education, 19*(1), 13-19.

Fosnot, C. & Dolk, M. (2012). *Young mathematicians at work: Constructing fractions, decimals, and percents.* Portsmouth, NH: Heinemann.

Gardner, H. (1999). *The disciplined mind.* New York: Simon & Schuster.

Hannaford, C. (2005). *Smart Moves: Why learning is not all in your head.* Salt Lake City: Great River Books.

Hannula, M. (2001). The metalevel of emotion-cognition interaction. In M. Ahtee, O. Björkqvist, E. Pehkonen & V. Vatanen (Eds.), *Research on Mathematics and Science Education. From Beliefs to Cognition, from Problem Solving to Understanding,* Institute for Educational Research (pp. 55-65). University of Jyväskylä.

Jones, K. (2001). Spatial thinking and visualization. In the report on *Teaching and learning geometry, 11-19,* 55-56. London, UK: Royal Society.

Krutetskii, V. A. (1976). *The psychology of mathematical abilities in schoolchildren.* Chicago: University of Chicago Press.

Lengel, T., & Kuczala, M. (2010). *The kinesthetic classroom: teaching and learning through movement.* Thousand Oaks, Calif.: Corwin.

National Council of Teachers of Mathematics (NCTM) (2014). *Principles to actions: ensuring mathematical success for all.* Reston, VA: NCTM.

Nesin, G. (2012). *Active Learning. This we believe in action: Implementing successful middle level schools* (pp. 17–27). Westerville, OH: Association for Middle Level Education.

Ontario Ministry of Education (OME) (2010). *Capacity Building Series: Communication in the mathematics classroom.* Toronto, ON: Queen's Printer for Ontario.

Presmeg, N. (2014). Creative advantages of visual solutions to some non-routine mathematical problems. In S. Carreira, N. Amado, K. Jones, H. Jacinto, (Eds.), *Proceedings of the Problem@Web International Conference: Technology, Creativity and Affect in mathematical problem solving* (pp. 156-167). Faro, Portugal: Universidade do Algarve, 2014.

Prince, M. (2004). Does Active Learning Work? A Review of the Research. *Journal of Engineering Education, 93,* 223-231.

Shoval, E. (2011). Using mindful movement in cooperative learning while learning about angles. *Instructional Science, 39*(4), 453-466. doi:10.1007/s11251-010-9137-2.

Vale, I., & Barbosa, A. (2018). *Gallery walk* uma estratégia para resolver problemas e promover discussões matemáticas produtivas. *Livro de atas do III Encontro Internacional de Formação na Docência (INCTE)* (pp.444-451). Instituto Politécnico de Bragança.

Vale, I., Barbosa, A., & Pimentel, T., (2016). Tarefas em contextos visuais e a formação de professores. In A. P. Canavarro, A. Borralho, J. Brocardo, L. Santos (Eds), *Investigação em Educação Matemática – Recursos na Educação Matemática* (pp. 83-86). SPIEM, 2016.

Vale, I., Pimentel, T. & Barbosa, A. (2018). The power of seeing in problem solving and creativity: an issue under discussion. In N. Amado, S. Carreira and K. Jones (Eds.), *Broadening the scope of research on mathematical problem solving: A focus on technology, creativity and affect,* (pp.243-272). Cham, CH: Springer, 2018.

Influence of activities with blocks on spatial visualization: gender difference in children aged 5 years [1]

Manuel Zenza [a], Pedro Palhares [a]

Elementary mathematics plays an important role in learning and is the basis for the development of a number of more advanced mathematical concepts. There are studies that suggest that the early tasks involving building with blocks are related to the spatial capacities of children.

There is also evidence of gender difference, and recent studies argue that such evidence begins from pre-school years, suggesting that use of programs involving space-related tasks in preschool may be more beneficial for girls than for boys. Based on these studies, the focus of our research was to examine the influence of activities using blocks on children's spatial visualization ability and to verify differences in performance between boys and girls. By analysing the results of the Pre-test and the Post-test, we verified that there were significant differences in gender performance only in the experimental group post-test, these being in favour of boys, who performed better than girls.

Introduction

Several studies have argued that children need to experiment and to solve spatial problems in order to ensure the development of simple space skills (Ponte, Brocardo and Oliveira, 2003). These experiences are fundamental for the development of the skills of perceiving changes in position,

---

[1] Zenza, M. & Palhares, P. (2020). Influence of activities with blocks on spatial visualization - gender difference in children aged 5 years. In G. S. Carvalho, P. Palhares, F. Azevedo, C. Parente, C. (Coord.), *Improving children's learning and well-being* (pp. 23-35). Braga: Centro de Investigação em Estudos da Criança / Instituto de Educação. ISBN: 978-972-8952-63-1

[a] CIEC, Institute of Education, University of Minho, Braga, Portugal.

orientation, and the size of objects, and at the same time they develop important geometric notions such as congruence, similarity and the transformation of figures (Mendes and Delgado, 2008).

Visualization in particular has always been considered an important component of mathematical thinking although, according to some studies, it has not always been given a prominent role in the mathematical experiences of children in areas other than geometry (eg, Presmeg, 2006).

Thus, geometry is often relegated to the background and when such subjects are addressed, concern is focused on the identification of forms and their attributes, rather than on spatial visualization (Clements, 2004).

A study by Wolfgang, Stannard and Jones (2001) suggests that tasks of building with blocks are related to spatial capacity. Also, several researchers have looked at pre-school children with regard to block games and have concluded that the geometrical properties inherent in blocks influence the development of logical-mathematical and spatial thinking in young children (eg, Ness and Farenga, 2016).

Gender differences are consistently reported in multiple visuospatial tasks, with men generally performing better in mental rotation tests, while women perform better in memory tests involving the location of objects. Although some studies on gender spatial capacity differences suggest that such spatial capacity is innate, there are other studies indicating that this difference can be eliminated through training and practice (Kocijan, Horvat and Majdic, 2017 and Zambrzycka, 2014).

Given the importance of construction activities with manipulatives for the future learning of mathematics, it is imperative that the teacher or educator provides diverse experiences in different contexts and with multiple materials that provide environments conducive to learning and experimentation (eg, Escorial e Castro, 2011 Verdine et al., 2014). This perspective led us to reflect on the relevance and importance of conducting a study addressing these issues.

Visualization

Defined by some as an internal or external representation of an object, and by others as the ability to form mental representations of the appearance of objects and to manipulate these representations in the mind, this terminology is not used in an agreed manner, and, in the field of investigation, such names as "spatial perception", "spatial imagery", "images", "spatial vision", etc. have been used (eg, Fernández, 2011, Hegarty and Kozhevnikov, 1999)

At 5 years of age, the child has a visualization capacity that allows him or her to reproduce a model placed before him or her or even when it is shown and then withdrawn (Owens, 2015). The child is also able to explicitly represent several reference points and the distances between them, to determine or remember locations and to interpret or create simple space models (NRC, 2009).

Spatial visualization may reflect a greater involvement of boys than girls in spatial activities. Boys often spend more time playing with Lego and making puzzles than girls. Boys tend to be more interested in movement and action from the first year of life and girls are more focused on social interactions. There are differences in the mean performance level between boys and girls in tasks of mental rotation at four and a half years of age, ranging from small but significant differences to large differences (NRC, 2009).

According to Halpern and Collaer (2005), a set of studies carried out in recent decades has revealed substantial gender differences in some, but not all, in terms of the processing of visuospatial information. As in verbal and quantitative abilities, the size and direction of gender difference depends on the specific test or task that is used, or more precisely, on the cognitive components needed to accomplish it. The many questions about gender differences in cognitive abilities are socially and politically sensitive due to the potential misuse of scientific results to fuel prejudice and discrimination. We note here that gender differences are found in a wide range of cognitive tasks, sometimes favouring women (for example, there is a substantial feminine advantage in writing tests and language fluency, many learning and memory tests, and a smaller, but significant advantage in mathematical computation), and sometimes favouring men (eg, most visuospatial tasks as well as quantitative problem solving tests).

Activity with blocks

Children's block building has been investigated for more than a century and its relevance is still present today. In pre-school settings, it is customary for children to have small blocks of wood of varying shapes and sizes for free activity purposes. Sometimes children are also required to copy a model or image in more difficult tasks that require symbolic representation. This construction activity is often recognized as an effective way of promoting children's overall development, literacy skills, social skills, mathematical abilities and spatial capacities (Tian et al., 2018).

Block activities can allow children to practice decomposing blocks and structures into components, recognizing that, for example, larger blocks and block constructs are made up of smaller units, since breaking a whole into units is not something that children do naturally. In addition, blocks are relatively accessible and block-building activities can be structured as a cooperative social activity that facilitates the use of spatial language among children and between children and their educators. There are two main types of block activities - free and structured. In free activities, children receive blocks and then build structures of their own choosing, invoking the imagination and the ability to produce complex relationships without stimulus. In structured activities, children try to make a particular structure from a given model. In this type of activity, children develop the ability to analyse spatial representation and then reproduce a predefined model (e.g., Verdine et al., 2014).

Block activities are important for the development of spatial visualization and allow children to practice block decomposition and component structures (NRC, 2009). According to McCormick and Twitchell (2017), pre-school children love to build; they build with large blocks, small blocks, blocks of wood, unit blocks, forms of magnetic construction and other types. Building blocks support children's learning in shape-shaping and shape-building and help develop key spatial capabilities.

Objectives of the study

Given the importance of visualization and of construction activities with manipulative materials for the future learning of mathematics, and based on the evidence presented by several researchers in this respect, the main objective of this study was to evaluate the effects of introducing a program of activities of the construction of shapes, including puzzles and patterns, in the spatial visualization capacity of 5-year-old children. In particular, on the basis of the evidence on gender differences presented by several researchers on this subject, even suggesting that the inclusion of spatial tasks in pre-school may be more beneficial for girls than for boys (Levine et al., 1999; Reilly, Neumann and Andrews, 2017), we decided to include gender differences in our study.

With the focus on this goal, throughout the investigation children were induced to engage in activities that involved the resolution of construction problems with manipulable blocks and the establishment of generalizations in visual contexts, by using the representation of forms, puzzles and patterns the same or similar to the model presented. In addition, a key feature of this study was to investigate if there is gender difference in the performance of the girls and the boys in exploratory problems using manipulable blocks.

Methodology

Two pre-school classes participated in this study, these being from two institutions of Social Solidarity from the Porto district. The choice of classes did not comply with a previously established criterion, but only with the objective that they should be made up of children who were the same age (5 years - unfortunately, we had one child of 4 years), that is, it was an aim that the two classes should have characteristics as close as possible, regarding the homogeneity of age or performance of the children and the surrounding context of both the school and the community. Thus, after careful consideration of the study objectives and the emerging implications of the data collection and analysis phases, we chose to involve the two existing groups (A and B) of 14 children each (6 boys and 8 girls and 7 boys and 7 girls respectively).

In order to achieve these objectives, we chose a Mixed Research design, framed in a Pragmatic Paradigm and integrating two methodologies (Quantitative and Qualitative). This type of research is at an intermediate point between the two paradigms (Positivist / Post-positivist and Constructivist), appropriate for this type of diversified approach and for evaluating objective and subjective knowledge. (Creswell, 2003, Tashakkori and Teddlie, 2003)

In the first phase of the study, associated with the Quantitative Methodology, a "Design with Non-Equivalent Control Group *" was chosen.

0_1	X	0_2
0_3		0_4

* Non-equivalent group design

This type of design was the most realistic, since:

a) The two groups were already formed and it was not possible to exclude the 4-year-old child from the study;

b) The researchers were not able to select the participants for the study, nor to perform a random distribution of the participants;

c) A pre-test was used to demonstrate the initial equivalence of the existing groups, relative to the dependent variable (visualization ability).

d) The groups were first compared in terms of results, as well as age, to ensure that the groups were equivalent.

e) The Experimental Group (14 children = 6 boys + 8 girls) and the Control Group (14 children = 7 boys + 7 girls) received the same pre-test and post-test;

f) The results of the tests were analysed using the covariance analysis procedure - ANCOVA (Coutinho, 2011).

Discussion

Advancing to the inferential analyses, this method allowed us to compare the groups of subjects who presented significant differences with respect to a pre-existing variable, regardless of whether the group was selected according to a qualitative variable, such as gender. Following this logic, if the independent variable is gender, then we are necessarily in the presence of two groups, one male and one female (Pinto, 1991).

In an attempt to test the effectiveness of the program in improving the effective performance of children in a spatial performance test, the differences in the mean values of children's performance in the pre-test and in the post-test were assessed according to gender in order to check for any significant differences (see following table). Using the test of homogeneity of variances (Levene's test), it was verified that in the experimental group there was an equality of variance in the means obtained by boys and girls in the total pre-test score ($F = 0.064$, $p = 0.805$) and in the score in the post-test ($F = 0.176$, $p = 0.683$). Similarly, in the comparison group, there were equal variances in the means obtained by boys and girls in the total pre-test score ($F = 0.371$, $p = 0.554$) and in the total post-test score ($F = 1,018$, $p = 0.333$).

		Sex	N	M	DP	t	Gl	Sig
Experimental group	Total Pre-test	Male	5	31.400	7.470	-.049	11	.962
		Female	8	31.625	8.383			
	Total Post-test	Male	5	53.800	11.120	2.207	11	.049*
		Female	8	38.000	13.310			
Comparison group	Total Pre-test	Male	7	21.000	4.633	-.054	12	.958
		Female	7	21.143	5.670			
	Total Post-test	Male	7	25.143	3.625	.529	12	.606
		Female	7	23.857	5.305			

Table 1. *Analysis of the difference of means in the groups according to gender*

After analysing the results recorded in this table, we were able to verify that there were significant differences according to gender only in the performance of children in the post-test of the experimental group. These significant differences in performance between boys and girls are in favour of boys who have a higher average performance (Mboys = 53,800> Girls = 38,000).

We must stress that differences in gender performance occur only in the post-test of the experimental group, and may lead us to reflect on the program we implemented and its impact for boys and girls.

In this study, the execution of the experimental activities with blocks was analysed taking into account the level of accuracy or success of the children in the reproduction of a model of a structure with blocks and (See Graph below), it was verified that, although they were at the same level in the tasks of puzzle-building and pattern-making, there were differences in shape building tasks, with boys performing better than girls.

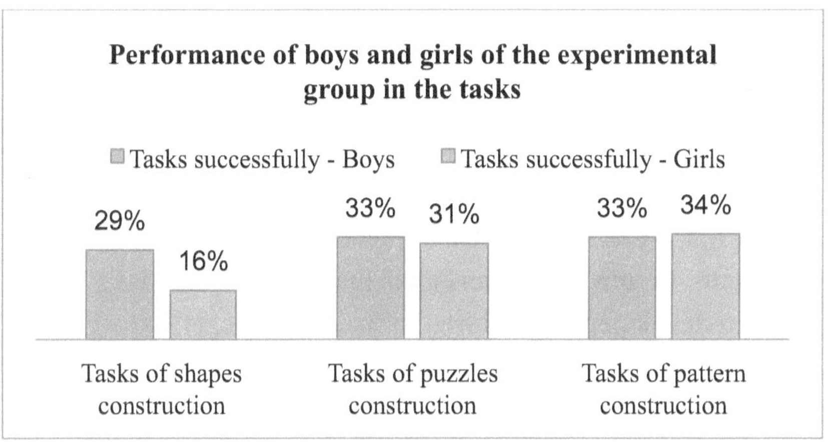

Graph: Global performance of boys and girls from the experimental group

After analysing the results of the experimental tasks and the results of the post-test, it was found that female children, although showing a slight improvement in pattern-making tasks (see Chart above), remain at a disadvantage compared to boys, especially in solving shape-building tasks.

Conclusion

Gender differences, in different cognitive domains, are often discussed, both scientifically and by the lay public. Both the research results and the researchers' own opinions vary with regard to gender differences at the beginning of mathematics learning. Some studies did not reveal gender differences in math performance. Other studies found differences favouring boys.

Focusing on the experimental group of this study, we tried to find out if there are differences of performance between boys and girls, either in the tests of spatial visualization or in the experimental activities of constructing shapes with blocks, including puzzles and patterns.

While the results of some studies suggest that the use of spatial tasks in pre-schools may be more beneficial for girls than for boys (eg, Levine et al., 1999; Reilly et al., 2017), the results presented in this study indicate that the experimental program applied is not the most effective for girls. Girls see their results, either in the experimental activities (mainly in the tasks of shape construction) or in the post-test, below the results obtained by the boys. Contrary to the evidence advocated by some researchers, the results of this study revealed that not all the tasks of the program developed for children in the experimental group of this study were equally beneficial for girls and boys.

In view of this conclusion, perhaps for a future investigation, the question arises: "What spatial tasks may be beneficial for both girls and boys in a program of development of visualization and mathematical education in general?"

References

Clements, D. H. (2004). Geometric and spatial thinking in early childhood education. In D. H. Clements, J. Sarama & DiBaise, M. A. (Eds.), *Engaging young children in mathematics: Results of the conference on standards for pre-school and kindergarten mathematics education* (pp. 267–298). Mahwah, NJ: Lawrence Erlbaum Associates.

Coutinho, C. P. (2011). *Metodologia de investigação em Ciências Sociais e Humanas: Teoria e Prática*. Coimbra: Edições Almedina.

Creswell, J. (2003). *Research Design: Qualitative, Quantitative and Mixed Methods Approaches*. London: Sage.

Escorial, B. & Castro, C. (2011). La gran torre: Matemáticas en la Educación Infantil a través de un proyecto de construcción. *Números. Revista de Didáctica de las matemáticas, 78,* 135-156.

Fernández, M. T. (2011). *Una aproximación ontosemiótica a la visualización y el razonamiento espacial*. Tesis Doctoral, Área de Didáctica da Matemática. Universidade de Santiago de Compostela: Faculdad de Ciencias da Educación, Departamento de Didáctica das Ciencias Experimentais.

Halpern, D. F. & Collaer, M. L. (2005). Sex Differences in Visuospatial Abilities. In P. Shah & A. Miyake (Eds.), *The Cambridge Handbook of Visuospatial Thinking* (pp.170-212). New York: Cambridge University Press.

Hegarty, M. & Kozhevnikov, M. (1999). Types of visual-spatial representations and mathematical problem solving. *Journal of Educational Psychology*, 91, 684–689.

Kocijan, V., Horvat, M. & Majdic, G. (2017). Robust sex differences in jigsaw puzzle solving. Are boys really better in most visuo-spatial tasks? *Frontiers in Behavioral Neuroscience*, 11, 194.

Levine, S. C., Huttenlocher, J., Taylor, A. & Langrock, A. (1999). Early sex differences in spatial skill. *Developmental Psychology, 35* (4), 940-949.

McCormick, K. K. & Twitchell, G. (2017). A preschool investigation: the skyscraper project. *Teaching children mathematics, 23*(6), 341-348.

Mendes, M. F. & Delgado, C. C. (2008). *Geometria: Textos de Apoio para Educadores de Infância.* Lisboa: DGIDC.

National Research Council (2009). Mathematics Learning in Early Childhood: Paths Toward Excellence and Equity. C. Cross, T. Woods, and H. Schweingruber (Eds). Center for Education, Division of Behavioral and Social Sciences and Education. Washington, DC: National Academy Press.

Ness, D. & Farenga, S. J. (2016). Blocks, Bricks, and Planks: Relationships between Affordance and Visuo-Spatial Constructive Play Objects. *American Journal of Play*, 8 (2), 201-227.

Owens, K. (2015). *Visuospatial reasoning: An ecocultural perspective for space, geometry and measurement education.* New York: Springer.

Pinto, A. C. (1991). *Psicologia Experimental: Temas e Experiências.* Porto: Edição do Autor.

Ponte, J. P., Brocardo, J. & Oliveira, H. (2003). *Investigações Matemáticas na Sala de Aula.* MG, Belo Horizonte: Autêntica Editora.

Presmeg, N. (2006). Research on visualization in learning and teaching mathematics: Emergence from psychology. In A. Gutiérrez e P. Boero (Eds.), *Handbook of research on the psychology of mathematics education* (pp. 205-235). Dordrecht: Sense Publishers.

Reilly, D., Neumann, D. L. & Andrews, G. (2017). Gender differences in spatial ability: Implications for STEM education and approaches to reducing the gender gap for parents and educators. In M. S. Khine (Ed.), *Visual-Spatial Ability: Transforming Research into Practice* (pp. 195-224), Switzerland: Springer International.

Tashakkori, A. & Teddlie, C. (2003). The past and future of mixed methods research: From data triangulation to mixed model designs. In A. Tashakkori & C. Teddlie (Eds.), *Handbook on mixed methods in the behavioral and social sciences* (pp. 671-701). Thousand Oaks, CA: Sage Publications.

Tian, M., Deng, Z., Meng, Z., Li, R., Zhang, Z., Qi, W., Wang, R., Yin, T. & Ji, M. (2018). The impact of individual differences, types of model and social settings on block building performance among Chinese preschoolers. *Frontiers in Psychology*, 9 (27).

Verdine, B. N., Golinkoff, R. M., Hirsh-Pasek, K., Newcombe, N. S., Filipowicz, A. T. & Chang, A. (2014). Deconstructing building blocks: preschoolers' spatial assembly performance relates to early mathematics skills. *Child Development*, 85(3), 1062-1076.

Wolfgang, C. H; Stannard, L. L. & Jones, I. (2001). Block play performance among preschoolers as a predictor of later school achievement in mathematics. *Journal of Research in Childhood Education,* 15 (2), 173-180.

Zambrzycka, J. (2014). Improving Preschoolers' Mathematical Performance: The Nature of Spatial Input by Early Childhood Educators. Master's thesis. Retrieved from http://scholars.wlu.ca/etd/1656, a 19 de Abril de 2018.

Financial education and mathematics in early years: a pedagogical proposal [1]

Lina Fonseca [a], Adriana Araújo [a]

Due to citizens reduced financial literacy it is the school's desire to provide them with knowledge through Financial Education (FE) and so to enable them to analyse situations and make appropriate and conscious, financial decisions. Since mathematics is present in an individual's life, the goal of the study was to interconnect these areas. It aimed to understand how 1st year pupils deal with money and improve their financial literacy, with the specific goals: a) identify previous ideas about money; b) familiarize pupils with coins and notes; c) understand the meanings of spend, save and donate; d) identify difficulties; and e) understand the effects of the didactic proposal. A qualitative methodology and explorative study were followed. The data gathering used participant observation, interviews, photos, tasks and pupils' documents. The results showed that: pupils initially had appropriate ideas about money, which were then developed; pupils managed to identify coins and give equivalent values; and they understood the meanings linked to the concepts of spend, save and donate.

Financial literacy

The situation of the financial crisis that our country, and other European countries, are seeing would by itself justify the

[1] Fonseca, L. & Araújo, A. (2020). Financial education and mathematics in early years: a pedagogical proposal. In G. S. Carvalho, P. Palhares, F. Azevedo, C. Parente, C. (Coord.), *Improving children's learning and well-being* (pp. 36-51). Braga: Centro de Investigação em Estudos da Criança / Instituto de Educação. ISBN: 978-972-8952-63-1

[a] Polytechnic Institute of Viana do Castelo, Viana do Castelo, Portugal.

need to embrace the challenge of providing financial education for children and young people, from an early age. But the problem is actually global.

In a globalized and free consumer society, inadequate financial literacy makes citizens more prone to economic difficulties, over-indebtedness, and family failures (OECD, 2016). It has become necessary to improve citizens' knowledge of financial matters, in order to enable them to select appropriate options, by being rightly informed. Small wrong financial decisions can have a lasting impact on individuals, their families and society.

According to OECD (2013), financial literacy is the knowledge and understanding of financial concepts and risks, as well as the capacities, motivation and confidence to apply that knowledge, and understanding to make effective decisions in a range of financial contexts, which will thus improve individual and social financial well-being and will enable individuals to participate in economic life. Similarly, Schagen, 1997, quoted by Banco de Portugal, 2011, says that "[Financial literacy] is the capacity of making informed judgements and concrete decisions with the aim of managing money" (p. 16).

In these two definitions of financial literacy, the making of decisions is stressed. For decisions to be effective and concrete it is necessary for individuals to own knowledge, to be properly informed and to develop their capacities to act in order to keep themselves financially healthy, and "to have access to information about products and services available to them" (Insurance Europe, 2017, p.19).

The first area for the improvement of knowledge, and the development of capacities and attitudes which promote a healthy relationship with money, can be the family. This, understood as a central nucleus for educating children financially, is a priority space for examples and reflections about the use of money. However, through the evolution of society, we know that not all children and young people have family contexts and relations that allow them to structure this learning. Thus, it is a role of the school, as a common space, democratic and attended by all, to reflect the desire to enable the new generations by promoting a financial education, from the early years of schooling. The school must contribute to develop pupils' financial literacy, one of the essential literacies for the 21st century (World Economic Forum, 2015), in a way such that all citizens can behave adequately to their financial situation and so avoid financial and social exclusion.

Financial education

Financial Education is abstract for children and pupils in the first years of schooling, and it can be argued that learning about it should be postponed to adolescence. However, children are consumers from an early age, and nowadays a great gap can be found between children and their knowledge of money, expenses, and saving and their sense of the value of money.

Financial education is the method by which the child creates bases to be able, in the future, to establish a healthy, balanced and responsible relationship with money (D'Aquino, 2008).

For the OECD (2005) financial education can be defined as the process by which financial consumers/investors improve their understanding of financial products, concepts and risks and, through information, instruction and/or objective advice, develop the skills and confidence to become more aware of financial risks and opportunities, to make informed choices, to know where to go for help, and to take other effective actions to improve their financial well-being (p.4)

For an informed, active and critical citizenship, it is necessary to create school learning environments which challenge the pupils to participate in the exploration and accomplishment of their ideas, to look for knowledge, to solve problems and to work in a group, developing capacities and positive attitudes (Fonseca & Leal, 2018).

Preparatory themes for Financial Education can be treated during the initial levels of schooling, such as is referred in the *Referencial de Educação Financeira* (REF) (MEC, 2013b). In this document, themes, subthemes and contents to work with are outlined, from kindergarten to secondary school and even into adult education.

The REF (MEC, 2013b) proposed themes are planning and budget management; systems and basic financial products; savings, credit and ethics; and rights and duties. The way each theme is treated, and its degree of depth are decided by the educator or teacher, adjusting them to their pupils.

Financial education themes, being abstract, need to be adapted to the children, even from the first years of schooling and, preferably integrated into the different curriculum areas, particularly mathematics.

Mathematics in primary schools

Mathematics is a central curricular area in primary schools. At the start of schooling, pupils develop their knowledge of numbers and the numeric system, basic operations (addition and subtraction), and they meet concepts of geometry, and measure and begin to deal with quantities, mainly money (MEC, 2013a).

Along with these aspects of programme content, they must develop their capacity to solve problems, communicate, argue in favour of their decisions, and think critically (Martins, et al. 2017).

Money is one of the quantities studied which is difficult for the pupils, because a direct comparison between any two quantities cannot be easily visualized (Ponte & Serrazina, 2000). It is necessary to find artefacts that allow an indirect comparison and that contribute to the pupils showing understanding of the mathematical concepts, besides procedural fluency (NCTM,

2014).

Taking the opportunity to work with a group of eleven pupils in their 1st year of schooling, it was decided to focus on the numbering system and quantities of money, as the beginning of the approach to Financial Education.

The study

In this study the intention was to understand how pupils in their 1st year of schooling dealt with money, when they had a low knowledge of natural numbers, and to increase their financial literacy. The main goals of the study were: (1) to identify pupils' previous ideas/conceptions about money; (2) to familiarize the pupils with coins and some notes of the monetary system; (3) to understand the meanings assigned by pupils to the concepts: spend, save and donate; (4) to identify the difficulties expressed by the pupils about the proposed tasks; and (5) to understand the effects of the didactic proposal on the knowledge shown by the pupils.

To achieve the proposed aims a didactic proposal was built, having as its base the *Programa de Matemática do Ensino Básico* (MEC, 2013 a) e o REF (MEC, 2013 b).

The following aspects relating to Financial Education were addressed: (a) to know that the Euro is the official currency of Portugal and other European countries and that there are other currencies, connecting them to the respective countries; (b) to establish the difference between *need* and *want*; (c) to make a distinction between necessary and superfluous expenses, and to give examples; (d) to relate saving to the possibility of the acquisition of goods and the attainment of long-term targets, (e) to understand currency as a means of payment; and (f) to simulate payments and give change in notes and coins (MEC, 2013b).

Having defined the aims, the study followed a qualitative methodology. In this qualitative approach of research, the descriptive and interpretative method, with an exploratory aim, was followed (e.g. Bogdan, & Biklen, 1994; Lessard-Hébert, Goyette, & Boutin, 2005; Coutinho, 2014). The exploratory investigation is usually conducted in new areas of research, as was the case here.

The participants formed a class of the 1st year of schooling and were pupils of six or seven years of age. At the start of this study, the pupils only knew the natural numbers up to 8, the vowels and the consonant P.

To collect data, tasks that formed the didactic proposal were used, namely: participant observation; interviews; photos; and documents from the pupils. The didactic proposal was formed of four tasks: Task 1- Students previous ideas about money (Money history); Task 2 – Contact with coins – identification and relations; Task 3 – Pocket money – "Little market"; Task 4 – Spend-Save-Donate.

Some results

The results for each task will be presented following the description of the task proposed to the pupils.

Task 1- Pupils' previous ideas about money (Money history)

The first task began with a story related to the weekly allowance and the value of money (Figure 1).

After listening to the story pupils talked about the ideas presented, particularly about the idea of weekly allowance and expressed correct ideas.

Teacher: What is a weekly allowance?

Pupil 11: Money?

Teacher: Who gives the weekly allowance?

Pupil 11: Parents.

Pupil 3: Grandfathers.

Pupil 5: Uncles.

Teacher: But what is a weekly allowance after all?

Pupil 11: It is money for the week.

Figure 1. *Money history*

They knew about the existence of euro coins and notes and some of their characteristics. They also knew that in other countries (e.g. Angola, United Kingdom) there are different currencies because they have relatives living there.

Teacher: Does anyone know money?

Pupil 10: Some is brown, other is euro.

Pupil 11: It's a coin and a note.

Teacher: Very well. We have coins and notes.

Teacher. What coins do you know?

Pupil 11: Golden coin, black coin.

They had some ideas that a long time ago there were neither coins nor notes and before their existence people performed direct exchanges.

Teacher: Before little coins...

Pupil 11: They exchanged things.

Teacher: Can you explain that exchange of things?

Pupil 11: When they wanted to buy things in a shop, they gave things they liked.

Teacher: How was that? Give me examples

Pupil 11: They exchanged a vase...

Teacher: They exchanged the vase for what?

Pupil 11: Ahhh... for a blanket.

This task was for these pupils the first step in financial education, which according to D'Aquino (2008) relates to the knowledge and manipulation of coins.

Task 2 – Contact with coins – identification and relations

It was then necessary to continue with the recognition and identification of coins and notes and to establish the value relations between them To help the pupils to overcome this task a challenge was created: every day, each child took coins randomly from a box and had to identify them. The results were registered on a table placed in the classroom (Figure 2).

Figure 2. *Coins to identify and table of the answers*

Some pupils showed great difficulty in telling the cent coins from the 1- and 2-euro coins. To help them with this distinction it was shown to them that coins of 1- and 2-euro were "coins with a crown". With this, they progressed more easily in the identification of coins, although slowly. A lot of persistence was necessary.

Next, it was necessary to relate coins to notes and coins to other coins. This was found to be very difficult for these pupils at the beginning of their schooling. Manipulative materials were used to help pupils to compare different coins (Figure 3), relating coins to bars of different dimensions, in a way that they could confirm that, for example, 1 euro is equivalent to 2 coins of 50 cents and to ten coins of 10 cents.

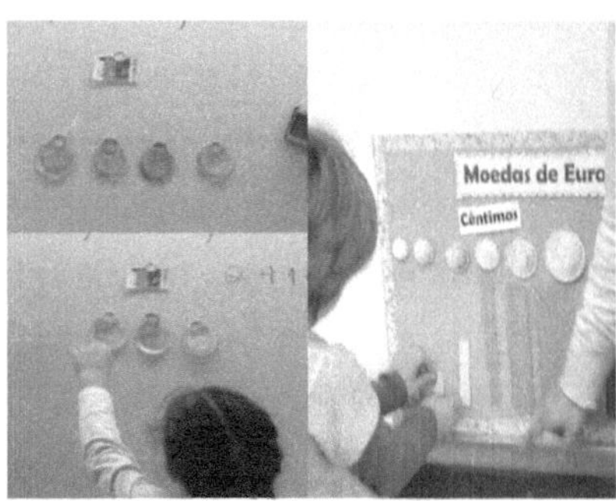

Figure 3. *Change a 5 € note for 1€ and 2€ coins. Comparison between 0,01€ and 0,02€*

Besides manipulative materials, games were created to use entertainment in the learning of money: a memory game, a game to identify the total value of the presented coins, a game of comparison and a game of sorting. These games helped pupils to gradually overcome difficulties with the identification of, and the relation between, different euro coins.

Task 3 – Pocket money – "Little market"

This task was designed with the aim of permitting the pupils to experience what would allow them to distinguish and to understand the concepts of "necessary" and "superfluous", to deal with the matter of saving. It is said that, for pupils at this age level to understand the need for saving, it is necessary that they have the possibility of spending! Only in face of concrete situations, they can decide freely an essential item for Financial Education - to save or not to save.

A "Little market" was created in the classroom. Pupils could buy school materials, sweets, accessories, games and toys. All products were marked with a price that the pupils of the 1st year of schooling could read and understand. To give them the possibility to frequent the "Little Market", a weekly allowance was assigned to them.

Every Monday each pupil received 5 coins of 20 cents - fictitious coins, of course. They had to decide what to buy, to check the price of each product and to verify if they had enough money for the purchase. After this was done, they had to address the teacher saying what they wanted to buy, the total price and the value of the change, when appropriate.

Figure 4. *Weekly allowance and "Little market"*

To encourage saving, some products in the "Little market" cost more than the pupils could afford each week.

Task 4 – Spend – Save – Donate

Linked with Task 3 was Task 4. It was important to develop in the pupils an attitude of attention to others, to the well-being of the other children. So, linked with the "Little market", the following rule was created: the 5 coins received weekly had to be put in 3 containers: one relative to Spend, other to Save and the third to Donate. They had to put at least one coin in each container. Each child had 3 containers and could distribute their coins freely, according to the rule (Figure 5).

All coins in the Spend container could be used immediately each week on Wednesday; the coins in the Save container could only be used at the end of May; the coins in the Donate container would be collected till the end of May and the pupils would decide to whom or to what institution they would like to offer goods and what goods they would like to donate.

Figure 5. *Each pupil containers for Save – Spend – Donate*

At first pupils put more coins in the Spend container and chose candies, sweets and chocolates. We could tell that some products in the "Little market" were tempting the children! And they were!

They were tempted at first. Afterwards they began to understand that if they wanted a more expensive object and could not afford to buy it immediately because of the lack of money, they needed to save for some time. They understood this clearly and changed the strategy. This change is visible in Figure 6.

One pupil (Pupil 7, Figure 6) had always spent as many coins as possible, maintaining an unchanging behaviour. He invariably chose candies. In contrast, we had two pupils (Pupil 3 and Pupil 8, Figure 6) who never put 3 coins in the Spend container.

In the end, when they could buy with the *money* they had saved, they opted almost unanimously for school materials they needed for their daily lives, like pencils, pens, and notebooks.

Caixa / Aluno	Spend box				Save box				Donate box				Total		
	23/11	07/12	04/01	11/01	23/11	07/12	04/01	11/01	23/11	07/12	04/01	11/01	(1)	(2)	(3)
Aluno 1	1	1	1	1	2	1	1	1	2	1	1	1	10	5	5
Aluno 2	1	2	1	2	2	1	1	1	2	2	1	2	8	5	7
Aluno 3	2	1	2	1	2	1	1	1	1	1	2	2	6	7	7
Aluno 4	2	1	2	1	2	1	1	1	1	1	2	1	10	5	5
Aluno 5	1	1	1	2	2	2	1	2	2	2	1	1	7	7	6
Aluno 6	2	2	2	1	2	2	2	1	2	1	1	1	9	6	5
Aluno 7	1	1	1	1	1	1	1	1	1	1	1	1	12	4	4
Aluno 8	1	1	2	1	2	2	1	2	2	2	2	2	5	7	8
Aluno 9	2	1	2	2	2	1	1	1	1	1	2	2	9	5	6
Aluno 10	2	1	2	1	2	1	2	1	1	1	1	1	8	8	4
Aluno 11	1	2	1	2	2	1	1	1	2	2	1	2	8	5	7

Legend:

	2 coins
	1 coin
	3 coins
	Same number of coins
	More coins
	Less coins

Figure 6. *Pupils' options for the distribution of weekly allowance*

The children learned how to deal with the fact of not being able to buy what they want when they want! They need effort and patience to reach their goals.

In order to enable pupils to develop their mathematical knowledge about the numbering system and money, the decision about donation took place at the end of the school year. The pupils gathered all coins that each one had put in the Donate container. After counting and organizing the 20 cents coins in groups of five, to make up 1 Euro, they counted 12 euro and 80 cents. What to do? A large group discussed it and they decided to spend the sum buying school material still existing in the "Little Market". What for? Another necessary decision. They then decided unanimously to donate it to the children of the school with financial needs who, for that reason, did not always have the materials they needed in the classes.

Figure 7. *Donated material*

This material was delivered to the school coordinator who was in charge of handing it out.

Conclusions

At the end of the study it is possible to conclude that the pupils showed correct previous ideas/concepts about money, specifically: (a) that there were coins of different colours and various notes; (b) that coins had changed over the years; (c) that before the modern euro coins, other different coins had existed; (d) that in other countries coins were different; and (e) they justified the need for money as a means of payment because of the direct exchange constraints.

During the didactic proposal, the pupils became acquainted with the coins and some notes of the monetary system. This matter turned out to be very complex for these pupils in the first year of schooling and at the beginning of the school year. The major difficulty was to discern 1 and 2 cent coins from 1 and 2 euro ones (D'Aquino, 2008; Ponte & Serrazina, 2000). The strategy of showing the latter as "coins with crown" was found to be useful and adequate. The manipulative materials were also found to be extremely useful in helping pupils to establish the values and equivalence relations of the different coins. The pupils' major difficulties were enhanced by their very limited knowledge of numbers, the numbering system, and their reduced capacity for conveying ideas.

The pupils assigned correct meanings to the concepts spend, save and donate, because they had practised them. This kind of action showed itself to be suitable for the learning of these themes by pupils in their 1st year of schooling. It also enabled them to distinguish the concepts of necessary and superfluous, as well as to practice saving, as defined in the reference *Ministério da Educação e Ciência* (2013b).

Since one of the essential aspects of Financial Education is to enable citizens to make informed decisions, it should be noted that these decisions were made by 1st year school pupils and that they decided to put part of their weekly-allowance in the Donate container and also that they decided what to donate and to whom (OECD, 2005).

Final remarks

Individual financial literacy has a slow development because it implies reflections on actions and decisions to make. To start with Financial Education in the beginning of basic schooling seems to be an adequate option for a school which is concerned to help pupils to deal with money and make informed decisions, as not all of them are part of structured families who can help them with this goal.

However, there are some aspects to be considered nowadays. Most of the children do not run errands for the families, such as shopping for small items in the local shops, which could let them meet real money. Also, in most schools' pupils don't deal with real money, because they only use a card. They deal with virtual money. The card is charged by parents or the education organisation responsible and the pupils cannot see money *disappearing*! Sometimes they do not even know how much they have spent. They only know if they have or have not money in the card!

These cards used in schools, although very functional,

should, when used in reading machines, enable pupils to see the amount of money they have spent and how much they still have. This could happen if images of existing and disappearing coins could be seen as they spend them. This could be an additional means of analysing options to balance their small expenses.

References

Araújo, A. (2016). *Educação Financeira desde a Infância: proposta didática para o 1º ano de escolaridade.* Relatório Final de prática de Ensino Supervisionada do Mestrado em Educação Pré-escolar e Ensino do 1º Ciclo do Ensino Básico. Escola Superior de Educação do Instituto Politécnico Viana do Castelo.

Banco de Portugal (2011). *Banco de Portugal, Comissão do Mercado de Valores Mobiliários e Instituto de Seguros de Portugal divulgam as linhas de orientação do Plano Nacional de Formação Financeira.* https://www.bportugal.pt/pt-PT/OBancoeoEurosistema/ComunicadoseNotasdeInformac ao/Paginas/combp20110517.aspx

Bogdan R., & Biklen S. (1994). *Investigação Qualitativa em Educação: Uma introdução à teoria e aos métodos.* Porto: Porto Editora.

Coutinho, C. P. (2014). *Metodologia de Investigação em Ciências Sociais e Humanas: Teoria e Prática.* Coimbra: Edições Almedina.

D´Aquino, C. (2008). *Educação Financeira. Como Educar o Seu Filho.* Rio de Janeiro: Elseviver.

Fonseca, L., & Leal, S. (2018). Planear com alunos do 3.º e 4.º anos de escolaridade. Contributo para o desenvolvimento do sentido de número. *Indagatio Didactica*, 10 (4). http://revistas.ua.pt/index.php/ID/article/view/11538

Insurance Europe (2017). *Financial education in a digital age. Initiatives by the European insurance industry*. Brussels: Insurance Europe aisbl.

Lessard-Hébert, M., Goyette, G., & Boutin, G. (2005). *Investigação Qualitativa. Fundamentos e Práticas*. Lisboa: Agence d'ARC.

Martins, G., Gomes, C., Brocardo, J., Pedroso, J., Carrillo, J., Silva, L., Encarnação, M., Horta, M., Calçada, M., Nery, R., & Rodrigues, S. (2017). *Perfil dos Alunos à Saída da Escolaridade Obrigatória*. Lisboa: Ministério da Educação/Direção Geral da Educação.

Ministério da Educação e Ciência (2013a). *Programa de Matemática do Ensino Básico*. Lisboa: Direção Geral da Educação.

Ministério da Educação e Ciência (2013b). *Referencial de Educação Financeira*. Lisboa: Direção Geral da Educação.

NCTM (2014). *Principles to Actions: Ensuring Mathematical Success for All*. Reston, VA: NCTM.

OECD (2016). *Financial education in Europe. Trends and recent developments*. Paris: OECD Publishing. http://dx.doi.org/10.1787/9789264254855-en

OECD (2013). *PISA 2012 Financial Literacy Framework*. OECD: Assessment and Analytical Framework.

OECD (2005). *Recommendation on Principles and Good practices for Financial Education and Awareness*. https://www.oecd.org/finance/financial-education/35108560.pdf

Ponte, J., & Serrazina, L. (2000). *Didática da Matemática no 1º ciclo*. Lisboa: Universidade Aberta.

World Economic Forum (2015). *New Vision for Education. Unlocking the Potential of Technology*. Geneva: WEF.

Primary school health education: how children can learn about microbes and hand hygiene[1]

Paulo Mafra [a,b]*, Nelson Lima*[a,c]*, Graça S. Carvalho*[a]

In a technologically advanced and globalizing world, it is necessary to adjust the curricula and teaching methodologies so that scientific training can be applied to the real and current situations of pupils' personal and social lives, thus contributing to improving their scientific literacy. The experimental teaching of science allows a better understanding of the children's world. Primary school children's natural curiosity is a gateway for better learning about microorganisms. Experimental primary school teaching of microbiology, focusing on hand hygiene, was implemented in this study. This practical activity was developed in Bragança, Portugal, with 16 pupils enrolled in the 4th year of primary school, by addressing the problem-question: "Why should you wash your hands before meals?" The results showed that pupils had come to recognize that they had bacteria on their hands and had verified the effectiveness of the hand washing process. It was concluded that this activity can help children as early as the primary school, through an autonomous and responsible manner, to understand the importance of hand washing, so that they see this procedure as not being just a socially correct behaviour or a simple rule to fulfil.

[1] Mafra, P.; Lima, N.; Carvalho, G. S. (2020). Primary school health education: how children can learn about microbes and hand hygiene. In G. S. Carvalho, P. Palhares, F. Azevedo, C. Parente, C. (Coord.), *Improving children's learning and well-being* (pp. 52-63). Braga: Centro de Investigação em Estudos da Criança / Instituto de Educação. ISBN: 978-972-8952-63-1
[a] CIEC, Institute of Education, University of Minho, Braga, Portugal.
[b] School of Education, Polytechnic Institute of Bragança, Bragança, Portugal.
[c] CEB – Centre of Biological Engineering, University of Minho, Braga, Portugal.

Introduction

In the world we live in, information is increasingly globalized and society is becoming ever more technologically advanced. This fact dictates that citizens should have an increasingly scientific training adapted to the new requirements, right from early in their schooling (Pedrinaci, 2012). Therefore, it is necessary to adjust curricula and teaching methodologies in such a way that scientific training can be applied to real and current situations of pupils' personal and social lives, thus contributing to their effective scientific literacy (Sanmartí et al., 2011), so that pupils can understand that the knowledge that circulates in the classroom can be transferable to their everyday lives (Pro, 2012; Lupión & Prieto, 2014). Indeed, experimental science teaching develops children's handling capacities and reasoning, allowing a better knowledge of the world that surrounds them (Sá & Varela, 2007; Harlen, 2007, Oliveira, 2010). In addition, several authors (Charpak, 2005; Partridge, 2006; Harlen, 2007; Martins et al., 2007) further argue that experimental science activities in basic education allow children to carry out important cross-curricular learning in terms of reading, comprehension and oral and written expression, mathematics and general thinking. In this sense, the importance of practical and experimental work is now widely recognized in basic education as an essential component of science education. When carried out in an atmosphere of freedom in communication and respect for the opinions of others, it can introduce situations that encourage children to talk, to communicate, to discuss ideas, to describe, to interpret and challenge the results of observations, to learn and to use words to explain and sort out their own ideas (Harlen, 2007; Varela, 2009).

The subject of microorganisms can be explored as early as the first years of schooling, using experimental teaching (Mafra & Lima, 2009; Byrne, 2011; Mafra, 2012; Faccio et al., 2013; Mafra et al., 2015; Mafra et al., 2016; Ruiz-Gallardo & Paños,

2017). The natural curiosity of primary school children is a gateway to the occurrence of learning that leads pupils to a better understanding of microorganisms. In Portuguese primary schools, this issue is not explicit in the program or in textbooks, although there is content that addresses this issue indirectly, or is associated with it (Mafra & Lima, 2009; Mafra et al., 2016).

Some studies have shown that children are able to learn about microorganisms from an early age (Carey, 1985; Byrne & Sharp, 2006; Byrne, 2011; Mafra, 2012; Ruiz-Gallardo & Paños, 2017). However, studies show that even after formal education many children continue to hold alternative ideas about the actions of microorganisms which seem to persist over time because many of these ideas are rooted in their imagination and fantasy and not in scientific evidence, making conceptual change difficult (Byrne, 2011; Mafra, 2012; Ballesteros et al., 2018). This suggests the need for an urgent change in the type of approach to this subject, preferably as early as possible in schooling.

In this sense, learning should include the development of practical work involving children in research processes. To this end, teachers need to know, through specific methodologies, what children already know, in order to challenge ideas previously presented and to ensure the progress of children in their learning, developing knowledge and understanding of the structure, functions and applications of microorganisms through both primary and secondary schools to ensure and maintain this progress (Byrne & Sharp, 2006; Byrne, 2011; Mafra, 2012; Ruiz-Gallardo & Paños, 2017).

This chapter focuses on the design of activities that can promote primary school pupils learning about microorganisms and associating them with healthy habits. The activity presented here has been planned and implemented in the classroom and describes a learning unit on microbiology teaching, helping to improve the understanding of issues related to the presence of microorganisms on pupils' hands and the recognition of the effectiveness of the hand-washing process.

Methodology

Design of the experimental script

Following the form and methodology of Martins et al. (2008) but adapting it to the topic of microorganisms, the activity was planned according to the following four sections: a) national curriculum; b) purpose of the activity; c) activity script for the teacher; d) activity script for the pupils. In this work, only (a) the national curriculum and (d) the script for pupils is presented.

National curriculum

The curricular framework of the activity was analysed in the program of the primary school (ME, 2001; ME, 2004), identifying sections (Table 1) in which the microorganisms issue is addressed indirectly, since it does not exist in a specific dedicated area (Mafra & Lima, 2009; Mafra et al., 2016).

Year	Program section of the primary school	Issue addressed / observations
1st	Section 1.Discovering Yourself. Point 4: The health of your body.	Recognition of hygiene standards for the body and food: *washing hands before eating*, cleaning teeth, washing food; the knowledge and implementation of their health surveillance standards (periodic visits to the doctor, personal health book).
2nd		*Daily hygiene habits*, the importance of drinking water, the shelf life of food, hygiene of spaces for collective use; recognition of the importance of vaccination for health.

Table 1. *Sections of the curriculum and the Environmental Studies program of the primary school (ME 2001, ME, 2004) (Underlining added by authors)*

Washing hands before eating is one of the topics in both 1st and 2nd school years, so this issue was used for experimental activities, aiming at the understanding of not only the need for this hygienic habit but also the existence of microorganisms on pupils' hands.

Script for the pupil

The script for pupils, in addition to presenting the problem-question (*"Why should you wash your hands before meals?"*), has three main parts:

- *Before the Experience* section, which presents the material to be manipulated and invites pupils to make predictions;

- *Experience* section, where the various steps to be carried out are explained together with spaces where pupils can record data resulting from their observations;

- *After the Experience* section, where pupils have a space to record their reflections on the results obtained and respond to the problem-question.

The script for the experimental activities is particularly useful in two ways: first, it supports the implementation of activities (both in its sequence and in nature); second, it allows pupils to record their observations, in the form of text, drawing and/or tables. In this way, the information given to pupils and obtained from them is registered in an organized way that helps pupils in responding to the problem-question initially posed.

This script activity aimed to support pupils in the experimental activities so that they would understand that they have bacteria on their hands and that effective hand washing reduces the number of microorganisms on their hands.

The activity started with the formation of four groups each of four pupils. Then, two Petri plates containing nutrient agar medium culture (5g/L peptone, 5g/L NaCl, 3g/L yeast extract and 15g/L agar as a gelling agent) were given to each group. One member of each group, before and after washing his/her hands, rubbed the Petri plates identified with "before washing hands" and "after washing hands", respectively. The Petri plates were placed on the window sill for two days. Pupils recorded their predictions about what they would observe after those two days. When this time had passed, they observed the Petri plates and recorded what they saw.

Participants

The activities were carried out with 16 pupils of the 4th year of a primary school in the town of Bragança, in Portugal. They were between 9 and 10 years old, eight male and eight female.

The pupils were organized into groups of four and carried out the experimental activities based on the script, taking as its starting point the problem-question enunciated in it. Throughout the activity, the pupils made predictions, observations, recordings and interpretations, which were later analysed and interpreted.

Results

After addressing the problem-question "*Why should you wash your hands before meals?*" the pupils recorded predictions about what they thought they would observe on the Petri plates two days after they had rubbed their hands on the respective dish, before and after washing their hands. Some representative pupils' predictions on "Before washing hands" Petri plates are shown below:

- *We will verify that there will be microbes (pupil G4);*
- *I think it will have many bacteria (pupil G2);*
- *I think colonies of bacteria will appear (pupil G1).*

And some predictions on the Petri plate "after washing hands":

- *There will be almost no microbes (pupil G4);*

- There will be no microbes (pupil G2);

- I think there will be a few bacteria (pupil G1).

It should be noted that the pupils had acquired the concept of microorganism/microbe/bacterium and its growth in Petri plates in previous activities such as in brushing teeth (Mafra et al., 2015), so they felt comfortable in giving this type of answer. After the registration of their predictions, pupils advanced to the conclusion of the experiment, following the script guidelines. The plates were contaminated by rubbing their hands before or after washing their hands and the results were observed after two days.

After two days, the "before hand washing" plates (A, Figure 1) of all groups had more bacteria colonies than those "after hand washing" (B). Pupils observed the existence of colonies on the plates (Figure 1) and drew them (Figure 2) in the script.

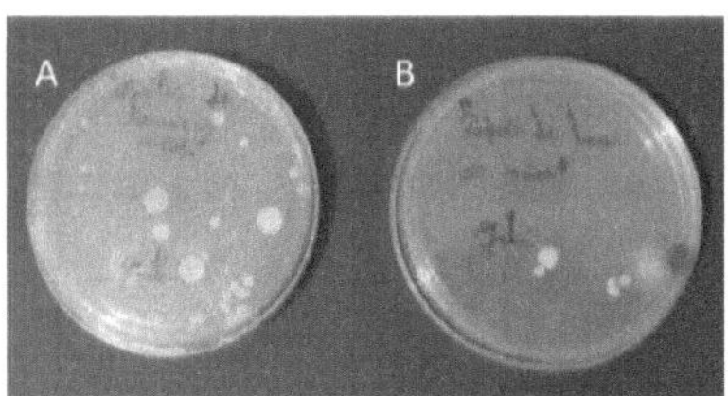

Figure 1. *Contaminated Petri plates before (A) and after (B) to washing hands*

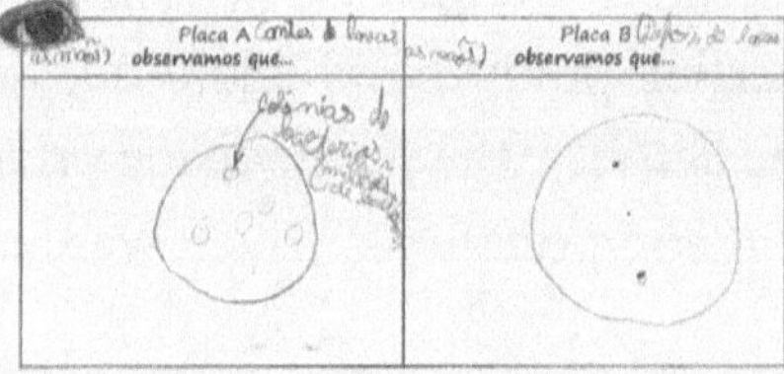

Figure 2. *Pupil's registration: plate A "before washing hands" and plate B "after washing hands"*

In the *After Experience* section ("We checked ...") of the script, they described what they observed. Some examples are the following:

- We found that plate A ["before washing hands"] had six colonies of bacteria and plate B ["after washing hands"] had none (pupil G1);

- We found that the number of bacteria decreased (pupil G3);

- We found that the "before hand washing" plate had more bacteria than the "after hand washing" plate. John had fewer bacteria because he had washed his hands before coming to school (G4 pupil).

Answering to the initial problem-question, some records were the following:

- We should wash our hands before meals so we do not swallow the bacteria with the food and will not get stomach ache (pupil G1);

- We must wash our hands because we can get serious diseases because we ingest bacteria (pupil G4).

In view of the answers given, and according to the discussion generated in the class, the children understood that "we have germs on our hands. However, if we wash them with soap and water (product used in this experiment), the amount decreases". Therefore, by answering the problem-question, they understood that they should wash their hands before meals to prevent microbes from being ingested with food and causing possible diseases.

Conclusion

The form of the script used allowed the children to carry out activities and arrive at an answer to the problem-question with relative ease. This experimental activity contributed to an improvement in the pupils' perception regarding the presence of microorganisms on their hands and the effectiveness of washing. Behaviours related to personal hygiene, other than hand washing, are now understood as behaviours related to the elimination of microorganisms harmful to health and not simply as a rule to be followed to fit in with social norms.

These results support the need for a change in the methodology for studying microorganisms at primary school. It is important for children to recognize, as early as possible, why they should adopt certain hygienic behaviours, providing meaning for such behaviour and thus contributing to the promotion of their health and to increase their scientific literacy.

Acknowledgments

This study was financially supported by Portuguese national funds through the FCT (Foundation for Science and Technology) within the framework of the CIEC (Research Center for Child Studies of the University of Minho) project under the reference UID/CED/00317/2019.

References

Ballesteros, M.I.; Paños, E.; & Ruiz-Gallardo, J.-R. (2018). Los microorganismos en la educación primaria. Ideas de los alumnos de 8 a 11 años e influencia de los libros de texto. *Enseñanza de las ciencias*, *36*(1), 79-98.

Byrne, J. (2011). Models of micro-organisms: Children's knowledge and understanding of micro-organisms from 7 to 14 years old. *International Journal of Science Education*, *1*, 1-35.

Byrne, J.; & Sharp, J. (2006). Children's ideas about micro-organisms. *School Science Review*, 88, 71-79.

Carey, S. (1985). *Conceptual development in childhood.* Cambridge, MA: MIT Press.

Charpak, G. (2005). *As ciências na escola primária: Uma proposta de acção.* Mem Martins: Editorial Inquérito.

Faccio, E.; Costa, N.; Losasso, C.; Cappa, V.; Mantovani, C.; Cibin, V.; Andrighetto, I.; & Ricci, A. (2013). What programs work to promote health or children? Exploring beliefs on microorganisms and food safety control behavior in primary schools. *Food Control, 33*(2), 320-329.

Garcia Barros, S.; Martinez Losada, C.; & Alonso, M. (1997). Estudiando las bacterias de la placa dental a través de una actividade práctica de investigación. *Alambique, 14*, 113-119.

Harlen, W. (2007). *Enseñanza y aprendizaje de las ciencias.* (3ª reimpresión da 2ª edición actualizada). Madrid: Ediciones Morata.

Jones, M.G.; & Rua, M.J. (2006). Conceptions of germs: Expert to novice understandings of microorganisms. *Electronic Journal of Science Education, 10,* 1-40.

Leite, L. (2001). Contributos para uma utilização mais fundamentada do trabalho laboratorial no ensino das ciências. In H. Caetano; M. Santos (Org.). *Cadernos Didáticos de Ciências* (pp. 77-96). Lisboa: Ministério da Educação, Departamento do Ensino Secundário (DES).

Lupión, T.; & Prieto, T. (2014). La contaminación atmosférica: Un contexto para el desarrollo de competencias en el aula de secundaria. *Enseñanza de las Ciencias, 32*(1), 1-18.

Mafra, P.; Carvalho, G.S.; & Lima, N. (2016). Os microrganismos nos programas e manuais escolares do 1.º e 2.º Ciclo do Ensino Básico português. *Gaia Scientia* (Edição especial Europa), *10*(2), 52-59.

Mafra, P.; Lima, N.; & Carvalho, G.S. (2015) Experimental activities in primary school to learn about microbes in an oral health education context. *Journal of Biological Education, 49*(2), 190-203.

Mafra, P. (2012). *Os microrganismos no 1.º e 2.º Ciclos do Ensino Básico: Abordagem curricular, conceções alternativas e propostas de atividades experimentais.* Tese de Doutoramento. Braga: Universidade do Minho.

Mafra, P.; & Lima, N. (2009). The microorganisms in the Portuguese National Curriculum and Primary School textbooks. In Mendez-Vilas, A. (Ed.), *Current research topics in applied microbiology and microbial biotechnology: proceedings of the International Conference on Environmental, Industrial and Applied Microbiology (BioMicroWorld2007), 2, Seville, Spain, 2007* (pp. 625-629). Hackensack: World Scientific Publishing.

Martins, I.P.; Veiga, M.L.; Teixeira, F.; Tenreiro-Vieira, C.; Vieira, R.M.; Rodrigues, A.V. & Couceiro, F. (2008). *Mudanças de estado físico. Guião didático para professores*. Lisboa: ME.

Martins, I.; Veiga, M.; Teixeira, F.; Tenreiro-Vieira, C.; Rodrigues, A.; & Couceiro, F. (2007). *Educação em ciências e ensino experimental. Formação de professores*. Lisboa: Ministério da educação.

ME - MINISTÉRIO DA EDUCAÇÃO (2001). *Currículo Nacional do Ensino Básico – Competências Essenciais*. Lisboa: ME - Departamento de Educação Básica.

ME - MINISTÉRIO DA EDUCAÇÃO (2004). *Organização Curricular e Programa: Ensino Básico – 1º Ciclo* (4ª edição revista). Lisboa: ME- Departamento de Educação Básica.

Oliveira, J. (2010). Contribuições e abordagens das atividades experimentais no ensino das ciências: reunindo elementos para a prática docente. *Acta scientiae, 12*(1), 139-152.

Partridge, J. (2006). Conducting a science investigation in a primary classroom. *Teaching Science, 52*(2), 44-45.

Pedrinaci, E. (2012). El ejercicio de una ciudadanía responsable exige disponer de cierta competencia científica. In Pedrinaci, E. (coord.), Caamaño, A., Cañal, P. & Pro, A. *11 Ideas clave. El desarrollo de la competencia científica*. Barcelona: Editorial Graó.

Pro, A. (2012). Los ciudadanos necesitan conocimientos de ciencias para dar respuestas a los problemas de su contexto. In Pedrinaci, E. (coord.), Caamaño, A., Cañal, P. & Pro, A. *11 Ideas clave. El desarrollo de la competencia científica*. Barcelona: Editorial Graó.

Ruiz-Gallardo, J.; & Paños, E. (2017). Primary school student's conceptions about microorganisms. Influence of theoretical and practical methodologies on learning. *Research in Science & Technological Education*, [Accessed in

20/10/2018]. Retrieved from https://www.researchgate.net/publication/320722030_Prim ary_school_students'_conceptions_about_microorganisms_ Influence_of_theoretical_and_practical_methodologies_on _learning.

Sá, J.; & Varela, P. (2007). *Das Ciências Experimentais à Literacia: Uma proposta didáctica para o 1.º ciclo*. Porto: Porto Editora.

Sanmarti, N.; Burgos, B.; & Nuño, T. (2011) ¿Por qué el alumnado tiene dificultad para utilizar sus conocimientos científicos escolares en situaciones cotidianas?. *Alambique: Didáctica de las ciencias experimentales, 67,* 62-69.

Varela, P. (2009). *Ensino Experimental das Ciências no 1º Ciclo do Ensino Básico: construção reflexiva de significados e promoção de competências transversais*. Tese de Doutoramento. Braga: Universidade do Minho.

The roulette of vaccines:
A didactic resource to approach Global Inequalities in Health Care Access with children [1]

Luísa Neves [a], Joana Oliveira [a], La Salete Coelho [a], Graça S. Carvalho [b]

There are still millions of people with no access to health care. Introducing this issue in education from the earliest years of schooling can contribute to raising public awareness about it and inspire actions to achieve the sustainable development goals, namely the SDG 3. To inspire teachers to do this, and aiming to make children feel what lack of healthcare access is like, and consequently to reflect on global inequalities on health care access, a board game was created. To assess its feasibility, this didactic resource was tested and discussed with teachers and educators involved in Global Citizenship Education. Results showed that it is feasible, it is adequate in familiarising children with the issue, it allows the achievement of the desired objectives, and it is adaptable for different ages and different contexts, both formal and informal, and in different countries. In addition, some of the participants considered that it could be adapted to other sustainable development issues like the access to clean water and access to education.

[1] Neves, L.; Oliveira, J.; Colho, L. S. & Carvalho, G. S. (2020). The roulette of vaccines: a didactic resource to approach Global Inequalities in Health Care Access with children. In G. S. Carvalho, P. Palhares, F. Azevedo, C. Parente, C. (Coord.), *Improving children's learning and well-being* (pp. 64-78). Braga: Centro de Investigação em Estudos da Criança / Instituto de Educação. ISBN: 978-972-8952-63-1

[a] High School of Education, Polytechnic Institute of Viana do Castelo, Portugal.
[b] CIEC, Institute of Education, University of Minho, Braga, Portugal.

Introduction

Education is central to the understanding of the world and should empower students to be active learners and, in the long run, to be able to intervene to improve the living conditions of their communities, so contributing to a more equitable and sustainable world. From a perspective of Global Citizenship Education, it is imperative to relate the curricular content, namely science-related concepts, to social issues and to stimulate the capacity for critical thinking and problem solving (Aikenhead, 2009; Europeen Comission, 2015; Hodson, 2003; UNESCO, 2010; UNESCO, 2016).

According to the Universal Declaration of Human Rights, particularly article 25th, everyone has the right to health and wellbeing (United Nations, 1948). Vaccination is a basic health care issue, with a great impact on the eradication of many infectious diseases and on the decrease of child mortality, which should be available to all. Yet, there are still millions of children with no access to this right. On the other hand, public controversies about children's vaccination in high income countries have arisen, where parents face conflicting information sources, from public health recommendations to risk-related information, so making it difficult for parents to decide on their children's vaccination (Colgrove, 2006; Ward et al., 2017). Introducing this issue into education from the earliest years of schooling can contribute to raising public awareness about it and inspire actions to achieve the sustainable development goals (SDG), namely "SDG 3: to ensure healthy lives and promote well-being for all at all ages", emphasising the importance of vaccination in improving public health (WHO, 2016; WHO/UNICEF, 2017).

To inspire teachers to transform their practices and connect the primary school curriculum and classroom context with global issues such as global inequalities, the European project *"Global Schools"* (involving 17 partners from 10 EU countries) has been set up to raise a new generation of world citizens motivated by values of solidarity, equality, justice, inclusion, sustainability and cooperation (*Global School*, 2015). Within the framework of this project, a handbook with didactic resources was developed, which includes a board game called "The roulette of vaccines" (Neves & Coelho, 2018; Neves et al, 2018).

The use of educational games *(i)* promotes children-children and teacher-children interactions, *(ii)* enhances children's social skills, such as communication and problem solving, *(iii)* increases motivation for learning, and *(iv)* facilitates the understanding of complex issues, such as vaccination (Gomes & Vilela, 2016; Kirikkaya, Iseri & Vurkaya, 2010; Liu & Chen, 2013). This specific game "The roulette of vaccines" aims to make children feel, and consequently reflect on, global inequalities in health care access and possible actions to transform the current situation. The aim of this paper is to describe this pedagogic game and discuss its potential for learning about global issues.

Description of the game "The Roulette of Vaccines"

"The roulette of vaccines" is included in Chapter 4 of the handbook mentioned above (Neves & Coelho, 2018; Neves et al, 2018), which addresses themes concerning health, poverty, inequality and social exclusion. It is part of a didactic sequence entitled "Health Step by Step", designed for primary school children. The choice of the topic of vaccination was based upon to the fact that:

(1) it is a very important and a not consensual social issue, opening space for the discussion of different points of view;

(2) it is urgent to raise awareness of the importance of vaccination for collective immunization;

(3) there are high asymmetries in health care access that must be addressed;

(4) it is a theme foreseen in the primary curriculum and children are familiar with it.

Game materials

The game includes a board (Figure 1), dice, counters, different types of cards (Budget, Health Centre, Passport, WHO and Hospital cards) and "Health Bulletins" with six vaccines to be completed (Figure 2).

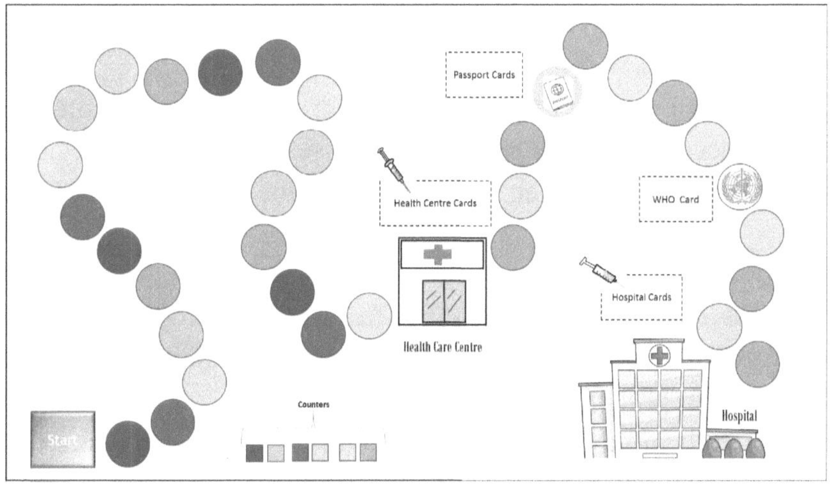

Figure 1. *Board of the game*

HEALTH BULLETIN	
Vaccine 1	Vaccine 2
Vaccine 3	Vaccine 4
Vaccine 5	Vaccine 6

Figure 2. *Health Bulletin*

Children are organized into six groups. Each group gets a "Health Bulletin" (Figure 2) and one card defining its budget and whether or not they have to pay for the vaccines, as follows:

- **G1** and **G5**: 900€ budget; has to pay for the vaccines;
- **G2** and **G6**: 400€ budget; has to pay for the vaccines;
- **G3**: 900€ budget; vaccines free;
- **G4**: 400€ budget; vaccines free.

The groups represent different countries:

- **G1** and **G2** – country A;
- **G3** and **G4** – country B;
- **G5** and **G6** – country C.

Before starting the game, the children should be questioned about vaccines, such as what are they useful for, which vaccines they know they had taken and where they got those vaccines.

Game rules

As each group represents different situations, according to the cards they have been given, the "rules" are slightly different for different groups:

1. All groups throw the dice and the group who gets the highest value starts to play. The game continues, taking turns, group by group, in a clockwise direction.

2. In turn, each group throws the dice and moves its counter the number of spaces indicated by the dice, with the aim of reaching the house that represents the Health Centre (it is not required to achieve the exact value; it can be higher).

3. Once at the Health Centre, each group picks up its Health Centre card.

4. Groups G1 and G2 pay 100 € for one vaccine which they then take at the Health Centre. They then get a signature on the Health Bulletin for the vaccine they have taken and start again from the beginning.

The G1 group will be able to buy more vaccines than G2 because it has more money available. The G2 group soon reaches a point where it cannot buy more vaccines because the does not have enough money.

5. Groups G3 and G4 take one vaccine in the Health Centre without paying.

Groups G3 and G4 are able to obtain all vaccines because vaccines are free for both groups, regardless of their starting budget.

6. When groups G5 and G6 get to the Health Centre, they will receive a card that explain that they should proceed to the main Hospital because the Health Centre does not have electricity to preserve the vaccines. Every time they roll the dice, they lose € 50 to pay for the trip.

Groups G5 and G6 have difficulty accessing vaccines, whether or not they have money to pay for the vaccines. They may face different situations: to emigrate to another country and find a different situation, to receive free vaccination in vaccination campaigns or to arrive to the hospital, paying for the trip.

If they land at the passport house they will pick a card from the top of the pile and emigrate to the country of groups G1 and G2 or G3 and G4 (depending on which card they take), returning to the beginning and assume their rules until the end of the game.

If they stop at he WHO house they will receive the WHO card:

the World Health Organization (WHO) is conducting a vaccination campaign near your home. You will receive a free vaccine and start again from the beginning.

When they arrive at the Hospital, they must take a hospital card from the top of the pile and follow the instructions. In the

Hospital, they will also face different scenarios: either they receive a free vaccine due to an organization's offer, or they have to pay for the vaccine, or they must wait because the hospital does not have vaccines at that time.

7. After taking a vaccine the groups must register it, through a signature, on their Health Bulletin and return to the starting house. Then they start the route again and continue the game until they have signatures for their entire vaccination report or the ones they can get with the money they have available.

8. Once a group runs out of money to access the vaccines, it exits the game.

9. The game ends when one of the teams has completed its Health Bulletin.

After the game proposed discussion

When the game is over, the feelings of the children while playing should be explored, and the concepts associated with the issue (different situations found in different countries and within the same country relating to health care access and the consequences), as well as possible solutions, should be discussed.

To promote the debate, teachers can use questions such as:

Q. How did the groups who were unable to complete their immunization record feel? And those who succeeded?

Q. In the country A, we found two different situations. What are they?

(G1 has money and can pay for all vaccines; G2 cannot afford all vaccines - access depends on money)

Q. In the country B, we also found two different situations. Can you identify them?

(G3 has money to buy all the vaccines and G4 has not, but both have access because there is a free health care system, so it does not depend on money)

Q. What are the situations in country C?

(G5 has money to buy all the vaccines, but G6 has money only for some of them. However, there are no vaccines accessible near home - access does not depend directly on the money, but on the availability and distance they need to travel).

Q. Why did some groups get more vaccines than others?

Q. If vaccines are not free for all, what can happen? Is it fair? What could we do to change this situation?

Q. How could you spend the remaining money?

Besides the issues arising directly from the game, the class can discuss other related issues as different vaccination plans for different countries and the importance of vaccination for collective immunization.

Testing the game with teachers

To assess the feasibility of the game "the roulette of vaccines", it was tested and discussed with teachers and educators involved in the *Global Schools* project, carried out in two workshops, one a national workshop with 10 participants and one international with 16 participants. After doing the game, participants were asked to answer some questions about what they thought of the game in terms of adequacy, usefulness and flexibility for adjustment to different contexts and groups, using a scale of 1 (not at all) to 5 (completely). The questions asked whether they would use it in their classrooms and why and what changes they would propose to enhance this pedagogical resource.

Results and discussion

The mean value of the teachers' answers to the adequacy of the game "The roulette of vaccines" in their classroom was 4.7, with a minor difference between Portuguese (4.8) and other teachers (4.6) (Figure 3). The usefulness of the game obtained a mean value of 4.8 in both groups (Figure 3). The mean value for the game's flexibility for use in different contexts and with different ages was 4.7 (Figure 3).

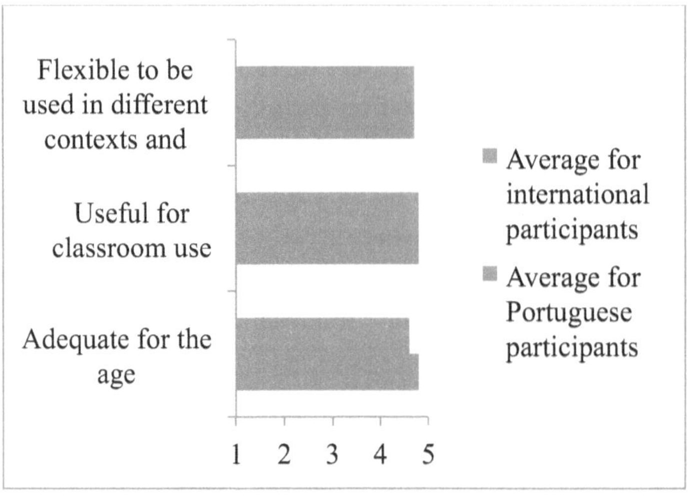

Figure 3. *Answers to the question: Too what extent do you consider the game adequate, useful and flexible? (1 - not at all to 5 – absolutely)*

In short, both Portuguese and international participants considered the game "The roulette of vaccines" to be adequate to the age of primary school children, useful for classroom work and flexible enough to be adapted to different contexts and different age groups.

Regarding the possible use of the game "The roulette of vaccines" in their classroom, most of the teachers responded "yes" (22 = 9 Portuguese + 13 International), mainly because they considered it to be flexible and fun, to provoke emotions and to promote reflection on global inequalities (Table 1). The reasons for not using the resource in their classroom, mentioned by four participants (1 Portuguese + 3 International), were mainly because they were not working at a primary school (Table 1).

These results show that most of the participants considered using the game "The roulette of vaccines" in their classroom, as well as in other educational contexts and felt that the game allows the achievement of the desired objective, which is to make children feel and reflect on health care access inequalities.

Yes	9 P	It is suitable for various ages, flexible to tackle different themes, etc. Alerts to existing inequalities. It is an educational resource that provides an approach to the theme "Access to healthcare" in a playful way. It helps students to realise that there are different realities according to the development state of the countries. It serves to sensitise children to the problem of poverty and lack of access to vaccination. It is also a way for children to better understand the distribution of goods. I think it's an activity that allows you to work on various themes. Because it helps to understand the importance of vaccination and to raise reflection around social problems.
	13 I	Good introduction to inequalities in access to health care within and between countries. I think it is a great tool. Fun activity, highlighting an important issue. Can be adapted to your own situation. It's very flexible and it can make children feel different contexts. It is adaptable to different age groups. Leads to discussion on fair/unfair, access/lack of access. Also engages emotions. Because this resource is flexible for many subjects. Because it's a really good and appropriate resource to show inequalities in health care access and pupils can have a global vision. Versatile. I find it a good starting point for discussion, a way to introduce other issues as well as health inequalities. I think it can be interesting to raise children's awareness on health issues, inequalities in the right to health (among others), equality of treatment. It could also be great in foreign language classes in secondary. It provokes emotions and further ideas. It starts from a "hot" theme heard by the students and can be

		treated in the various disciplines covering the curriculum.
No	1 P	I would apply it on contexts of no formal education.
	1 I	Because I am not a teacher, simply.
Oth ers	2 I	I don't teach at primary/secondary level, so I need to know the national curriculum requirements before answering this question. I would like to present it to my students, for discussion.

Table 1. *Answers to the question: Would you use "The roulette of vaccines" in your classroom? Why?*
P – Portuguese; I – International (Authors translated the answers written in Portuguese, Italian and French to English)

Data presented in Table 2 shows the participants´ suggestions to improve the proposed game "The roulette of vaccines". From the eleven answers, only one came from a Portuguese participant.

P	The possibility to share the money left over at the end of the game.
I	To make the game more playable, I would add more "passport points" to allow children to change their destiny (or at least try). I would not play with 6 players because my students are not so patient to wait a long round. Include new levels of difficulty with taxes. Making more space on the board if 6 people playing – hard for small fingers + manipulation. I would add more instructions and maybe a kind of explanation about each group instead of just saying "you have x money and you pay y for the vaccines"; something like life stories. And introduce gender perspective as well. More graphics on the board. Perhaps this is already in the handbook, but I would ensure that real stories are heard, included. Perhaps some research by the students so they also see realities of this issue. Bring more element of "gaming". Going there and back (in a circle)

	might cause loosing of attention. Choosing who can get the vaccination. This is just a comment, but it may be interesting to develop a similar game on access to clean water or clean aid (especially in the developing country context) or combine it with the issue of access to education. Not seen all suggested follow up questions but could ask how parents can decide what choice to make when not enough money + what can be done nationally, globally, link to access.

Table 2. *Answers to the question: Would you suggest any changes to the game "The roulette of vaccines"?*
P – Portuguese; I – International (Authors translated the answers written in Portuguese, Italian and French)

Analysis of these answers led to their organization in three categories: (1) design of the board; (2) dynamics of the game; and (3) other issues to be introduced (Table 3).

Data presented suggests that the game could be more appealing if the board is bigger and includes mores graphics. It also points to the inclusion of more gaming elements, as well as possibilities to make choices like who gets vaccination or about the sharing of money. In addition, some participants suggested introducing or using the game for other issues such as access to safe drinking water or access to education. The need to introduce more gaming elements and alternative paths is in line with the opinions of pre-service teachers who also had the opportunity to experience the game (data not shown).

Categories	Improvement proposals
Design of the board	More graphics on the board. More space on the board if 6 people playing.
Dynamics of the game	Fewer players because students are not patient enough to wait their turn in a long round. More "passport points" to allow children to change their destiny. More elements of "gaming".

	More instructions and maybe a kind of explanation about each group, like life stories. Possibility of choosing who can get the vaccination. Possibility of sharing money.
Other issues to be introduced	Introduce gender perspective. Combine it with the issue of access to education. Develop a similar game on access to clean water or clean aid.

Table 3. *Categories of improving the game "The roulette of vaccines"*

Final Remarks

To raise awareness about inequalities in health care access and the importance of vaccination for all, the Portuguese team of the *Global School* project proposed a pedagogical game named "The roulette of vaccines". Teachers and educators of different European countries who played and evaluated it, suggest that this pedagogical proposal is feasible, is adequate for introducing the issue to children, allows the achievement of the desired objectives, and is adaptable to different ages and different contexts, both formal and informal, and in different countries. In addition, this kind of game can be adapted to other issues like access to clean water or access to education. Further studies are required for testing the "The roulette of vaccines" in primary classrooms with children so that they discuss, analyse and provide further suggestions to improve the game.

References

Aikenhead, G.S. (2009). *Educação Científica Para Todos.* Mangualde: Pedago.

Global Schools (2015). *Global Schools.* Retrieved from http://www.globalschools.education/frontend/Project

Colgrove, J. K. (2006). *State of immunity: the politics of vaccination in twentieth-century America.* University of California Press. Retrieved from https://www.ucpress.edu/book/9780520247499/state-of-immunity

European Commission (2015). *Science Education for Responsible Citizenship*. Luxembourg: European Union.

Gomes, I.G.C. & Vilela, M. L. (2016). Recursos didáticos sobre a temática vacinação nos anos iniciais: diálogos possíveis entre a pedagogia e a biologia. *Revista de ensino da Biologia*, 9, 2507-2519.

Hodson, D. (2003).Time for action: Science education for an alternative future. *International Journal of Science Education*, 25:6, 645-670.

Kirikkaya, E.B., Iseri, S. & Vurkaya, G. (2010). A board game about space and solar system for primary school children. *The Turkish Online Journal of Educational Technology*, 9:2, 1-13.

Liu, E. Z. F. & ChenPo-Kuang (2013). The Effect of Game-Based Learning on Students' Learning Performance in Science Learning – A Case of "Conveyance Go". *Procedia. Social and Behavioral Sciences* 103, 1044 –1051.

Neves, L. & Coelho, L. (coord.) (2018). *Global Schools: propostas de integração curricular de Educação para o Desenvolvimento e Cidadania Global no 1º e 2º CEB*. Viana do Castelo: Escola Superior de Educação do IPVC. Disponível em http://portal.ipvc.pt/images/ipvc/ese/pdf/globalschools/maq uete_final_final_pages.pdf

Neves, L.; Esteves, A.; Barbosa, A.; Madeira, E.; Barbosa, G.; Oliveira, J.; Cardoso, J.; Coelho, L.; Gonçalves, T. (2018). Global schools: integração curricular da ED/ECG no ensino básico. In R. P. Lopes, M. Vara Pires, L. Castanheira, E. Silva (Eds.), *III Encontro Internacional de Formação na*

Docência (INCTE): livro de atas (pp. 850-859). Bragança: Instituto Politécnico de Bragança.

UNESCO (2010). *Current Challenges in Basic Science Education*. France: UNESCO.

UNESCO (2016). *The Global Education Monitoring Report team: Education for people and* planet: Creating sustainable futures for all. France: UNESCO.

United Nations (1948). *Universal Declaration of Human Rights*. Retrieved April 27, 2019, from https://www.un.org/en/universal-declaration-human-rights/

Ward, J. K., Crépin, L., Bauquier, C., Vergelys, C., Bocquier, A., Verger, P., & Peretti-Watel, P. (2017). 'I don't know if I'm making the right decision': French mothers and HPV vaccination in a context of controversy. *Health, Risk and Society*, 19(1–2), 38–57.

WHO (2016). *State of Inequality – Childhood immunization*. Switzerland: World Health Organization.

WHO/UNICEF (2017). Progress and Challenges with achieving Universal Immunization coverage. Available at https://www.who.int/immunization/monitoring_surveillanc e/who-immuniz.pdf

Auditory Processing Screening (APS) in children of school age [1]

Inês Martins [a], Cristiane Nunes [a], Simone Capellini [b], Graça S. Carvalho [a]

Auditory Processing Screening (APS) in children of school age is of great importance since it allows the early detection of difficulties in auditory competencies, anticipating or justifying possible difficulties in learning. APS was applied to 48 children aged 7-11 years. This study showed that among the three APS tests (SL, VSM and NVSM) the VSM was the most difficult test for the children since more than one-third of them (17 children or 35.4%) had scores below the expected figures. This study also showed that boys had significantly lower results than girls in the NVSM test. All children with below-expected RPA results should undergo a formal evaluation of Auditory Processing (AP) to explore the difficulties encountered.

Introduction

Hearing plays an important role in linguistic and cognitive development. It is through the perception of acoustic signals that communication develops and it is through this that dialogue between individuals can be established. This communicative interaction contributes to the development of several cognitive functions (Nunes, 2015).

[1] Martins, I.; Nunes, C.; *Capellini* S. & Carvalho, G. S. (2020). Auditory Processing Screening (APS) in children of school age. In G. S. Carvalho, P. Palhares, F. Azevedo, C. Parente, C. (Coord.), *Improving children's learning and well-being* (pp. 79-88). Braga: Centro de Investigação em Estudos da Criança / Instituto de Educação. ISBN: 978-972-8952-63-1
[a] CIEC, Institute of Education, University of Minho, Braga, Portugal.
[b] LIDA, Paulista State University, Marília, Brasil.

In addition to the detection of sound, it is essential that the sound can be interpreted and understood. Auditory Processing (AP) involves a set of competencies that are responsible for acoustic analysis: sound localization and lateralization, acoustic information sequence storage, discrimination, and identification of temporal aspects of sound in the presence of degraded and competitive acoustic signals (ASHA, 2005).

Problems in AP can be perceived through, among others, difficulties in learning, communication, speech or language (Ribas, Rosa &, Klagenberg, 2007; Santos, et al., 2015; Souza, Passaglio & Lemos, 2016). Given the importance of AP in cognitive-linguistic development, its evaluation is an important asset.

AP assessment can be done using formal or informal behavioural tests or screening. Screening tests can be applied as an indicator of risk for altered auditory processing, even in children younger than seven years old (Nunes, Pereira & Carvalho, 2012).

This specific study is a part of a larger research project for which the main objective is to evaluate and compare the auditory and cognitive-linguistic competences in school-age children. In this study, an Auditory Processing Screening (APS) set of tests was applied to school-age children to identify those with auditory difficulties.

Method

In the academic year 2017/2018, children of the 2nd, 3rd and 4th grades of primary education were evaluated using APS. Children with hearing complaints, such as the presence of auditory acuity deficits and children with an intellectual deficit, were excluded. In this way, a total of 48 pupils (18 of the 2nd grade; 15 of the 3rd grade; and 15 of the 4th grade) participated in the study. Their age range was between 7 and 11 years old, the breakdown being as follows: 9 children of 7 years old; 18

children of 8 years; 14 children of 9 years; 6 children of 10 years; and 1 child of 11 years. For data organisation, the 11-year-old child was included in the group of 10-year-old children. Of the 48 pupils, 19 were girls and 29 were boys.

The children underwent APS tests in a schoolroom, away from the areas with the most noise. Each student was evaluated individually.

The APS consisted of three auditory tests: SL - Sound Location Test (Pereira, 1993); VSM - the Verbal Sequential Memory Test (Toniolo, 1994) and NVSM - Non-Verbal Sequential Memory Test (Toniolo, 1994).

In the SL Test, the child was asked to locate the sound of a rattle in 5 different positions with reference to the head (above, back, front, left side and right side). The child had to remain seated with eyes closed during the test.

In the VSM test, the child had to be able to memorize and discriminate between sequences of verbal sounds in 3 different orders (syllables /pa/, /ta/, /ka/ and /fa/). At the end of listening to each sequence, he/she had to be able to repeat it orally.

In the NVSM test, the child had to be able to memorize and discriminate between sequences of nonverbal sounds, in 3 different orders (sounds of 4 instruments: rattle, agogô, bell and coconut). At the end of each sequence heard, he/she had to play the sounds in the order presented.

This NVSM test is important in the identification of the degree of risk for Central Auditory Processing Disorder and it can be applied in a context outside the acoustic booth (Nunes, 2015).

The expected scores, for APS, for the age group above 7 years are:
- LS tests - 4 correct answers out of 5;
- VSM test – 2 correct answers out of 3;
- NVSM - 2 correct answers out of 3.

Statistically significant differences between groups were analysed by using Levene's test and Student's *t*-test, at the confidence level of 95%. Descriptive parameters (frequencies, means, minima, maxima) were also analysed (Maroco, 2018).

Results

Children of the four age groups (7, 8, 9 and 10-11 years old) were analysed using the SL, VSM and NVSM tests and the results are shown in Tables 1 to 3, respectively. Table 1 shows that only three children (one per year group, but none for the 9-year-old group) had SL scores below the expected 4 correct answers. The remaining 45 children of all age groups had scores equal to or greater than 4.

Age	SL Test			
	Correct answers*			
	3	4	5	Total
7	1	2	6	9
8	1	1	16	18
9	0	2	12	14
10-11	1	0	6	7
Total	3	5	40	**48**

* Expected correct answers: 4

Table 1. *SL Test Results*

For the VSM test, of the 48 children, 35.4% (17 children (5+12); Table 2) of all age groups, obtained VSM scores below the expected 2 correct answers. The remaining 31 (20+11) children had scores equal to or greater than 2 (Table 2).

	VSM Test				
	Correct answers*				
Age	0	1	2	3	Total
7	0	1	5	3	9
8	3	4	8	3	18
9	2	5	4	3	14
10-11	0	2	3	2	7
Total	5	12	20	11	48

* Expected correct answers: 2

Table 2. *VSM Test Results*

For the NVSM test, Table 3 shows that of the 48 children, only a total of 5 for all age groups (none in the 7-year-old group), had NVSM scores below the expected 2 correct answers. The remaining 43 children had scores equal to or greater than 2.

	NVSM Test			
	Correct answers*			
Age	1	2	3	Total
7	0	4	5	9
8	3	6	9	18
9	1	2	11	14
10-11	1	2	4	7
Total	5	14	29	48

* Expected correct answers: 2

Table 3. *NVSM Test Results*

Table 4 pools together the results of the LS, VSM and NVSM tests showing the minimum, maximum and mean scores obtained in each children's group (7, 8, 9 and 10-11 years old) as well as the corresponding expected correct scores. The LS and NVSM mean scores obtained in all age groups were above the expected figures. In contrast, the VSM mean scores were lower than the expected ones in two groups (8 and 9 years old); the 7-

year-old and 10-11 year-old groups had results equal to or above the expected scores.

Age (years)	Number (N) and scores	APS		
		SL	VSM	NVSM
7	N	9	9	9
	Min.	3	1	2
	Max.	5	3	3
	Mean	**4,6**	**2,2**	**2,6**
	Expected	*4*	*2*	*2*
8	N	18	18	18
	Min.	3	0	1
	Max.	5	3	3
	Mean	**4,8**	**1,6**	**2,3**
	Expected	*4*	*2*	*2*
9	N	14	14	14
	Min.	4	0	1
	Max.	5	3	3
	Mean	**4,9**	**1,0**	**2,7**
	Expected	*4*	*2*	*2*
10-11	N	7	7	7
	Min.	3	1	1
	Max.	5	3	3
	Mean	**4,7**	**2,0**	**2,4**
	Expected	*4*	*2*	*2*
Total	N	48	48	48

Table 4. *SL, VSM and NVSM scores (min, max and mean) by age group and expected values*

No statistically significant differences (p>0.05) between age groups were found concerning each APS test, even after comparing merged groups, i.e. comparing the group of 7 plus 8 year-old children with the group of 9 plus 10-11 year-old children.

Table 5 shows the results of the LS, VSM and NVSM tests by children's sex. For the NVSM test, statistically significant differences ($p<0.05$) were found, girls having higher scores than boys, whereas no significant differences ($p>0.05$) were found between girls and boys scores in both LS and VSM tests (Table 5).

Tests	Sex	N	Mean	*P* value
LS	F	22	4,74	0,736
	M	32	4,79	
VSM	F	22	1,95	0,291
	M	32	1,66	
NVSM	F	22	2,84	0,001*
	M	32	2,28	

* Statistically significant differences at the level of 95%.

Table 5. *LS, VSM and NVSM scores by sex*

Conclusions and discussion

This study showed that among the three APS tests (SL, VSM and NVSM), the VSM was the most difficult test for the children since more than one-third of them (17 or 35.4%; Table 2) had scores below the expected value. In contrast, only a few children showed difficulties in the other two tests, SL and NVSM, with respectively 3 (6.3%, Table 1) and 5 children (10.4%, Table 3) below the expected scores. Similar results have been found with children with learning difficulties in reading and writing, where the VSM test was the one with the lowest results (Engelmann & Ferreita, 2009; Pelitero, Manfredi & Schneck, 2010). Thus, the present study suggests that the VSM test may be used to provide an alert for the need for further evaluation of AP in children already known to have literacy difficulties, as well as for the early identification of children with possible future learning difficulties.

This study also showed that boys had significantly lower results than girls in the NVSM test. Similarly, studies in the United States of America (Musiek and Chermark, 2007; Zampieri et al., 2019) and in Portugal and Brazil (Nunes, Pereira & Carvalho, 2012; Zampieri et al., 2019) have reported more boys than girls diagnosed with Auditory Processing Disorders. Since there is an association between the auditory processing difficulties and learning (Thomas, Kaipa & Ganesh, 2015; Zampieri et al., 2019), it is important to conduct an extensive evaluation of AP to rule out possible disorders. All children with lower results in APS should undergo a formal evaluation of AP to explore the difficulties encountered.

These are just preliminary results of a pilot test with a small sample of children. The subsequent screening study will be applied to a larger sample with at least 150 children to reinforce or counter these results. It is expected that the APS together with other instruments (central auditory processing instruments and cognitive-linguistic instruments) will be able to compare auditory and cognitive-linguistic skills and identify children with some signs of central auditory disorders or learning disorders.

Acknowledgements

This study was financially supported by Portuguese national funds through the FCT (Foundation for Science and Technology) within the framework of the CIEC (Research Center for Child Studies of the University of Minho) project under the reference UID/CED/00317/2019.

References

ASHA (2005). *(Central) Auditory Processing Disorders.* Retrieved from http://www.asha.org/policy/TR2005-00043/.

Engelmann, L., & Ferreira, M. I. D. C. (2009). Avaliação do processamento auditivo em crianças com dificuldades de aprendizagem. *Revista da Sociedade Brasileira de Fonoaudiologia, 14* (1), 69-74.

Maroco, J. (2018). *Análise estatística com o SPSS statistics (7th ed.).* Pêro Pinheiro: Report Number.

Nunes, C. L., Carvalho, G. S. de, & Pereira, L. D. (2012). A avaliação do processamento auditivo em crianças de 10 a 13 anos: sua função como indicador da perturbação da comunicação e do desempenho académico. (Doctoral Thesis, University of Minho, Portugal). Retrieved from https://repositorium.sdum.uminho.pt/bitstream/1822/22128/1/Cristiane%20Lima%20Nunes.pdf.

Nunes, C. L. (2015). *Processamento auditivo - conhecer, avaliar e intervir.* Lisboa: Papa-Letras.

Pelitero, T. M., Manfredi, A. K. S., Schneck, A. P. C. (2010). Avaliação das habilidades auditivas em crianças com alterações de aprendizagem. Revista CEFAC, 12 (4), 662-670.

Ribas, A., Rosa, M. R. D., & Klagenberg, K. (2007). Avaliação do processamento auditivo em crianças com dificuldade de aprendizagem. *Revista Psicopedagogia, 24* (73), 2-8.

Santos, T.S., Mancini, P. C., Sancio, L. P., Castro, A. R., Labanca, L., & Resende, L. M. (2015). Achados da avaliação comportamental e eletrofisiológica do processamento auditivo. *Audiology Communication Research, 20* (3), 225-232.

Souza, M. A., Passaglio, N. J. S., & Lemos, S. M. A. (2016). Alterações de linguagem e processamento auditivo: revisão de literatura. *Revista CEFAC, 18*(2), 513-519.

Thomas, R. M., Kaipa, R., Ganesh, A. C. Auditory interference control in children with learning disability: An exploratory Study. *International Journal of Pediatric Otorhinolaryngology, 79,* 2079-2085.

Zampieri, M. S., Tavares, J. R., Koury, G. V. H., Bigarelli, J. F. P., Ferreira, D. B., & Souza, I. C. N. (2019). Ocorrência de alterações do processamento auditivo em crianças com transtorno da aprendizagem. *Electronic Journal Collection Health, 11* (5), 1-11.

Quality of family life for children between the ages of 0 and 3 in a rehabilitation unit [1]

Bianca Valverde [a], Andrea Jurdi [a], Ana Paula da Silva Pereira [b]

Because of the importance of family participation, studies have been getting closer to the theme of the quality of family life, with the goal of improving the health care for children. This study has the goal of analysing the quality of family life of children between zero and three years old, who attend a rehabilitation unit of the public health service. The study involved the participation of the families of ten children with possible or present issues affecting their development, all cared for in the Specialized Center for Rehabilitation II in Santos, Brazil. The Family Quality of Life Scale was the data collection instrument used. Among the results found, we highlight the the fact that all the carers who participated were mothers, whether or not the mother had a job, the low level of school attendance and the variable relations with the quality of family life. It is hoped that this study will contribute to future research and actions on public health services focused on the family during the intervention process.

Introduction

Research into the quality of life in families which include children with Special Educational Needs (SEN) has shown a

[1] Valverde, B.; Jurdi, A. & Pereira, A. P. S. (2020). Quality of family life for children between the ages of 0 and 3 in a rehabilitation unit. In G. S. Carvalho, P. Palhares, F. Azevedo, C. Parente, C. (Coord.), *Improving children's learning and well-being* (pp. 89-107). Braga: Centro de Investigação em Estudos da Criança / Instituto de Educação. ISBN: 978-972-8952-63-1
[a] Federal University of São Paulo, Santos, Brasil.
[b] CIEC, Institute of Education, University of Minho, Braga, Portugal.

growing interest in this subject since the 2000's, and there have been a number of important theoretical studies about it (Correia & Santos, 2018; Ferreira, 2014; González, Centeno, Rueda, García, & Peral, 2015).

Current research studies look into the quality of family life in order to better understand the influence of family life quality on each family member, especially when one of them presents characteristics related to SEN. Based on this, it becomes possible to approach a better understanding of the influence of the potentialities and weaknesses of the context on the family's quality of life (Jorge, Levy, & Granato, 2015).

It is also important to consider that a complete and detailed analysis of the quality of life cannot be separated from the context where the persons live, and it must consider the interactions of the factors present in an actual situation (Schalock & Verdugo, 2002). In this sense, the quality of family life provides a fundamental contribution by developing this idea with a view to modifying the conceptions and the focus of public policies, influencing the way of thinking about the actions of the health care services to take account of the perspective of the families, and so acting as a guide in present and future efforts (Pérez, 2013; Schalock & Verdugo, 2002).

For many years, the study of human development reflected a "fragmented, linear and decontextualized vision, prevalent in this area of study" (Rossetti-Ferreira, 2006, p.20). However, the current tendency is to try and unite the complexity of development and its many dimensions, expanding the study of the individual to include their context and interactions with other family members, and to viewing different aspects of the human development.

Among the main authors to consider the human development through relations, Bronfenbrenner stands out by proposing a bio-ecological model. Initially named "ecologic", the bio-ecological theory suggests a system built upon inter-relations of socially organized systems that support and guide human development (Molinari, Silva, & Crepaldi, 2005). According to this model,

> the ecology of human development involves the scientific study of progressive, mutual accommodation, between an active human being, in development, and the mutating properties of the immediate environments in which the developing person lives, as this process is affected by the relations between these environments, and by the broader contexts in which the environments are inserted. (Bronfenbrenner, 1979, p.18)

According to Bronfenbrenner (1979), this context or "ecological environment" is composed of four subsystems namely: the microsystem (the context close to the developing individual, in which the activities pattern and the interpersonal relations happen), the midsystem (involving the relations between microsystems), the exosystem (involving the indirect influences of environments) and the macrosystem (broad socio-cultural relations). Therefore, following this line of understanding, human development is the result of a process of interactions between the child and the many contexts that encircle them, characterized by systems (family, groups, communities and societies) interdependent and inter-related with different levels of influence, situated in a specific time and space. This broad socio-historical context encompasses both culture and family organization, and cannot be limited to a strictly linear and causal vision of development. (Bairrão & Almeida, 2003; Molinari et al., 2005).

Early intervention centred on family and quality of family life

From the bio-ecological perspective, social interaction is an important element in human development, the family environment forming a central part of the network of relations of the child. In line with this, over the past few years studies have shown a growth in importance given to the participation of families in the programs of intervention in child healthcare

(Brichi & Oliveira, 2013; Carvalho et al., 2016). Many of these studies highlight the family environment and the relations with the child present in this context as facilitators of the rehabilitation processes (Formiga, Pedrazzani, Silva, & Lima, 2004; Sari & Marcon, 2008). Following this line, interventions in healthcare which do not include the context would be of limited value, since it is necessary to propose actions that also include the family and community, and it is not being possible to produce a universal model covering every individual and situation.

On this basis, the approach of early intervention centred on the family proposes that the practices developed with children with SEN or who are at risk should be made in the context of the child's family life. The family context is considered to be the main environment for the development of such children, providing an environment in which their competences are valued and their choices are respected (Bairrão & Almeida, 2003; Dunst, Bruder, & Espe-Sherwindt, 2014; Franco, 2007; Pereira & Serrano, 2014). Furthermore, this model tries to answer the needs of the individuals involved and to create opportunities for the development of the children based upon an active role by their families in providing the necessary support and resources. (Dunst & Bruder, 2002).

For such a proposal to become reality, it is necessary that both the practices of evaluation and intervention and the studies developed on this theme consider three fundamental aspects: the necessities and aspirations of the families, their functioning style and the resources that they provide for the care of a family member with SEN (Serrano, 2007).

In the current scenario, going beyond the identification of the development issues and the possibilities of intervention, some studies have demonstrated the importance of an approach centred on the family and its beneficial results in the interaction between the children and the family, seen in the well-being of the child and family satisfaction, as well as in the co-accountability between all involved. (Dunst, Trivette, & Hamby, 2007; Espe-Sherwindt, 2008; Serrano, 2007).

This approach to early intervention, established within a bio-ecological framework, is characterized by a change of focus from exclusive attention to the child to a focus centred on the whole family, encouraging their participation in the process.

For this to happen, it is fundamental to pay attention to the structure of an individual family considering their needs and priorities (Costa, Serrano, Dunst, Mestre, & Cañadas, 2017). It is worth considering that the family context frequently faces daily obstacles that make it harder for the family members to become involved with the development of the child, especially when the child has SEN (Bittencourt & Hoehne, 2009). Among these difficulties, key highlights include the large number of requirements and the greater need to provide support, which may put a family in a vulnerable position (Bailey et al., 2005; Coutinho, 2004).

Since the family is one of the contexts of importance for people with SEN, as they may depend on their families for support for longer in their lives, studies about the family quality of life are essential to discover their needs and capabilities. Therefore, the goal of this study was to analyse the quality of family life of children between zero and three years old with current or possible SEN.

Method

This paper is part of a research study that used a combination of quantitative and qualitative methods. In this paper we present the results of a quantitative study made using the Family Quality of Life Scale.

The Family Quality of Life Scale (FQOLS) (Hoffman, Marquis, Poston, Summers, & Turnbull, 2006) was used in this study with a cultural adaptation for Brazilian Portuguese. The scale was created and standardized based on a project undertaken in the USA with the goal of evaluating the quality of life in families that have children with general pathologies, through five domains: satisfaction of the individual about the family interaction, relationship between parents and children, emotional well-being, physical/material well-being, and support related to SEN (Jorge et al., 2015).

The scale comprises 25 items divided into five domains, namely: family interaction, parent-child relationship, emotional well-being and disability-related support. It has five types of satisfaction responses, rated on a Likert scale, where one stands for very dissatisfied, two for dissatisfied, three for neither satisfied nor dissatisfied, four for satisfied end five for very satisfied.

The study involved the participation of the families of ten children, between the ages of zero and three years old, with possible or present SEN, all cared for in the Specialized Center For Rehabilitation II in Santos, State of São Paulo, Brazil, and all enrolled in this service in the year 2017. The family members were invited to participate in the interviews voluntarily. These interviews were made individually between November 2017 and March 2018, in the healthcare unit.

For the data analysis, the names of participating family members were substituted by codes, from Family Member 1 to Family Member 10, to preserve their privacy. The data collected through completion of the FQOLS were noted, and, with the help of a statistician, were analysed through descriptive statistics, which makes it possible to "describe and evaluate a certain group, without extrapolating any conclusions or inferring anything about a larger group" (Peternelli, 2006, p.13).

To investigate the association between the domains of the FQOLS, as well as between these and the variables of family income and number of children in each family, we used the Pearson coefficient of linear correlation. To compare the domains of the FQOLS related to the variables of employment of family members and school enrolment of the child, we used the Student t test for non-related samples, with p ≤ .05 used as the criterion for statistical difference.

The research was submitted and approved by the Ethics Committee in Research with Humans from the Federal University of São Paulo. After clarifying the goals of the research, every participant signed an Informed Consent Term.

Results

Regarding the characterization of participants (Table 1), the ten family members that agreed to participate in the research were all females aged between 21 and 38, with an overall average age of 28.4 years. These 10 participants are mothers of the cared-for children, and these children were aged between 3 and 35 months, with an overall average age of 16.7 months. The family unit was composed of an average of 3.9 members, with a minimum of 3 and a maximum of 6 family members. The number of children varied between 1 and 4, with an average of 1.9. Also, among the family members, 60% were employed and 70% of the children were enrolled in school.

Family	Age of Family Member	Age of Child	Number of Children	Number of people in the family	Does the interviewed Family member have a job?	Does the child attend school?
Family member 1	32 years	35 months	1	3	Yes	Yes
Family member 2	38 years	4 months	3	5	Yes	No
Family member 3	22 years	31 months	1	3	Yes	Yes
Family member 4	33 years	25 months	4	6	No	No
Family member 5	30 years	32 months	2	4	Yes	Yes
Family member 6	25 years	4 months	2	4	Yes	No
Family member 7	33 years	3 months	1	4	Yes	No
Family member 8	25 years	7 months	3	4	No	No
Family member 9	21 years	7 months	1	3	No	No
Family member 10	25 years	19 months	1	3	No	No

Table 1. *Characterisation of mothers*

From the Family Quality of Life Scale (Table 2), the mean score of quality of family life was 3.83 (from 3.01 to 4.41). In the domains evaluated, the mean for the *family interaction* item was 3.91, for the *parent-child relationship* item 4.11, *emotional well-being* 2.95, *physical and material well-being* 3.70, and lastly, *disability-related support* 4.52. As it can be seen, disability-related support is the domain with the highest degree of satisfaction (mean = 4.52), while emotional well-being was the least satisfactory for family members (mean = 2.95).

Family	Family Interaction	Relation between parents and children	Emotional well-being	Physical and material well-being	Support related to disability	Total
Family Member 1	3,16	4,50	3,50	3,60	4,50	3,85
Family Member 2	4,83	4,66	3,50	4,60	4,50	4,41
Family Member 3	4,50	4,33	3,75	4,20	5,00	4,35
Family Member 4	2,33	3,50	2,00	3,00	4,25	3,01
Family Member 5	4,33	4,66	3,25	4,40	4,75	4,27
Family Member 6	4,00	3,66	2,75	4,20	4,50	3,82
Family Member 7	4,50	4,66	3,75	3,40	5,00	4,26
Family Member 8	3,00	3,50	2,00	3,80	4,25	3,31
Family Member 9	4,50	4,33	2,75	3,20	4,75	3,90
Family Member 10	4,16	3,66	2,25	2,60	3,75	3,28

Table 2. *Domains of family quality of life*

No strong correlations were observed between the domains of the Family Quality of Life Scale, neither of these with the variables family income and number of children. However, positive correlation was observed between families in which the family member interviewed works and the variables parent-children relationship (p = 0.036), emotional well-being (p = 0.001), physical and material well-being (p = 0.025) and total Quality of Family Life (p = 0.020). There was also a positive correlation between the families in which the child goes to school and the variable emotional well-being (p = 0.031).

Discussion

Even though the study is still in its final phase, it is clear that all the adult family members involved were female, the mothers of the children treated in the rehabilitation unit, and that 60% of those family members are employed, which gives us information about the role of these persons inside the family and with the healthcare processes.

The gender of the caretaker has been considered in the studies about family quality of life of persons with SEN, and it has been observed that the majority of the family caretakers who seem to deserve special attention are female, as they have a higher work load in the care tasks and become more restricted in their social activities (González et al., 2015).

For Fiamenghi Junior and Messa (2007), the family roles are defined through characteristics, ways of acting and premises established by the society in which this context is placed, leading to accepted norms in the way of performing these roles. In this scenario, despite the current changes regarding family structure, the role of the woman as mother is still central in the family and in the caretaking relation with the children. This aspect of the context can be observed in data presented about the participation of mothers, even though most of them are employed. This fact is related to the conception that the domestic tasks are still linked to the female role, as is the care between mother and children, despite the growing participation of women in the job market (Borsa & Nunes, 2011).

Apart from that, the exclusive participation of mothers in the survey corroborates what is observed in studies about the involvement in programs of intervention with children, in which women are observed as being the main caretakers, signalling the necessity of attention to the possibility of distress and work overload in some situations (Macedo, Silva, Paiva, & Ramos, 2015).

The results of this study also point to a positive relation between the employment state of the person interviewed and greater quality of family life, especially for the items emotional well-being, relation between parents and children, and physical and material well-being. Jorge (2011) also found a positive relationship between the family member being employed and the quality of family life, just like other studies that indicate increased sense of overload when related to the mother not being employed. Bronfenbrenner (1996) also describes that parents' work, although not actively including the child, is an exosystem with great influence on child development. Regarding the school environment, its strengthening as an ecological system is fundamental in view of its protective role as a social support network. This data points to the need and the challenge of reinforcing this context, including and expanding its performance considering it as an important point in the support network, child development and quality of family life.

It is also possible to highlight the positive relation between school attendance frequency and the item emotional well-being. This item is related to the satisfaction of personal interests, of stress relief and the presence of external help. This result is in line with evidence described by Schalock and Verdugo (2002) about the greater satisfaction of individuals when services of health or education are present in addition to support networks.

The school context plays an important role in the pathway to care in early intervention. According to Bronfenbrenner (1979), the school has a fundamental role in promoting child development, since the entry of the child in a new microsystem enables different relationships and experiences, enabling support for the child and promoting interaction between contexts. Although family members highlight the potential of relationships established at school and their importance in family support, the need for adaptation and fears regarding the child's insertion in the educational context are presented as major challenges.

These difficulties appear in school attendance, since it can be seen in the results of participant characterization that 70% of the children are not enrolled in a teaching unit, which is even more than that indicated by the 2015 school census, in which 48.05% of the children of Santos between 0 and 3 years old were not enrolled in day care (Fundação Seade, 2016).

Low school attendance goes against what is proposed by family-centred practices that understand school, in addition to the family environment, as a natural context in the inclusion of children with special needs by providing opportunities for social interaction and independence through everyday situations (Carvalho, 2016). Furthermore, it shows us that, although school inclusion is constantly being discussed, it is still necessary to rethink the contours of this institution, which often faces the lack of basic aspects to guarantee the inclusion and continuity of these students in school, evidenced by the contradictions of the policies related to the theme in this age group, which still do not highlight the place of disability in early childhood education.

In addition, another aspect identified as a challenge in the path to early intervention concerns the particular conditions of access to services and the possibilities of structural and routine organization of the family. According to Oliveira (2016), in his study on legal norms about early childhood in Brazil, public policies describe the idea of a universal childhood in which everyone has the same rights, without questioning the diverse conditions of access to them that each individual and his/her family find. Thus, the singularities of each context are missed, and it is necessary to approach the different forms of family organization, considering as well the relationships with the broader issues of the other systems – meso, exo and macrosystem – in order to embrace everyone and ensure full care and attention.

On the bio-ecological perspective of development, and specifically in the quality of family life, the microsystem and the exosystem have important impacts on the analysis of these relations. If the microsystem refers to the interactions inside the family context, the exosystem represents the contexts and the, relations with schools, health services or work and employment systems that are established with the family, and includes the degree of integration of services offered to the family, and how the community organizes itself to answer to the needs of children and their families (Serrano, 2007).

In this way, ecological systems and the community networks of support, formal or informal, have to be considered, with the goal of aiding the strengthening of these families, considering that all of them, "as long as they have the necessary support and resources, have conditions to positively promote the development of their children" (Carvalho et al., 2016, p. 81).

Final remarks

This study analysed the quality of family life of children between the ages of zero and three years, who attend a rehabilitation centre, through the FQOLS domains. Moreover, it also considered the connections of this data with the social reality in which these families live, seeking to reflect on the social, cultural and historical reality of the facts (Minayo, 2008).

In this context, it was noted that all those participating were female family members, despite the participation of some of these women in the job market, and that the school attendance frequency of the children involved in early intervention was low. Regarding the five domains studied, it was observed that there was a relation between the quality of family life and the employment of the family member interviewed, especially with regard to the domains emotional well-being, relation between parents and children, and physical and material well-being. There was also a relation between the children's school attendance frequency and the domain emotional well-being.

This data points to a need to consider the family roles and the gender of the main caretaker, as well as their involvement in the job market, in studies about family quality of life, in addition to the problem of initial inclusion and on-going continuity of children in the school system, considering its importance in the practices of early intervention centred in the process of strengthening families and enhancing their quality of life.

In this way, all the processes of healthcare intervention may benefit, opening a space for the empowerment of families and bringing more sensitivity to the care practices in public health services.

Considering all this, we hope that our study may contribute to future research, policy discussions in this sector and actions that focus on the family in the process of healthcare intervention.

References

Bailey, D. B., Hebbeler, K., Spiker, D., Scarborough, A., Mallik, S., & Nelson, L. (2005). Thirty-six-month outcomes for families of children who have disabilities and participated in early intervention. *Pediatrics*. 116, 1346-1352. doi: 10.1542/peds.2004-1239

Bairrão, J., & Almeida, I. C. (2003). Questões actuais em intervenção precoce. *Psicologia, 17*(1), 15-29. Retrieved from http://www.scielo.mec.pt/pdf/psi/v17n1/v17n1a01.pdf

Bittencourt, Z. Z. L. C., & Hoehne, E. L. (2009). Qualidade de vida de familiares de pessoas surdas atendidas em um centro de reabilitação. *Ciência & Saúde Coletiva. 14*, 1235-1239. doi: http://dx.doi.org/10.1590/S1413-81232009000400029

Brichi, A. C. S., & Oliveira, A. K. C. (2013). A utilização da abordagem centrada na família na reabilitação neuropediátrica. *Revista Brasileira de Ciências da Saúde. 11*, 74-81. Retrieved from http://seer.uscs.edu.br/index.php/revista_ciencias_sau de/article/viewFile/2006/1478

Borsa, J. C., & Nunes, M. L. T. (2011). Aspectos psicossociais da parentalidade: o papel de homens e mulheres na família nuclear. *Psicologia Argum.*, Curitiba, 29, 31-39. Retrieved from https://periodicos.pucpr.br/index.php/psicologiaargum ento/article/view/19835/19141

Bronfenbrenner, U. (1979). *The Ecology of Human Development: Experiments by Nature and Design.* Harvard University Press.

Carvalho, L., Almeida, I., Felgueiras, I., Leitão, S., Boavida, J., Santos, P., ... Franco, V. (2016). *Práticas recomendadas em Intervenção Precoce na infância. Um guia para profissionais* (1ª ed.). Coimbra: Associação Nacional de Intervenção Precoce.

Correia, R. A., & Santos, M. J. S. (2018). Qualidade de Vida Familiar na Deficiência Intelectual: Revisão Sistemática de Estudos. *Psicologia: Teoria e Pesquisa*, 34, 1-10. doi: https://dx.doi.org/10.1590/0102.3772e34414

Costa, C., Serrano, A., Dunst, C., Mestre, J. M., & Cañadas, M. (2017). Práticas Centradas na Família e os resultados familiares: avaliação de práticas de intervenção precoce na perspetiva da família. *Revista de Estudios e Investigación en Picología Y Educación*, Extr.(11), 274-278. doi: https://doi.org/10.17979/reipe.2017.0.11.3015

Coutinho, M.T. B. (2004). Apoio à família e formação parental. *Análise Psicológica*, 1, 55-64. Retrieved from http://www.scielo.mec.pt/pdf/aps/v22n1/v22n1a06.pdf

Dunst, C. J., & Bruder, M. B. (2002). Values outcomes of service coordination, early intervention and natural environments. *Council for Exceptional Children*, 68, 361-375. Retrieved from https://uconnucedd.org/wp-content/uploads/sites/1340/2016/06/ValuedOutcomesServCoord-2002.pdf

Dunst, C. J., Bruder, M. B., & Espe-Sherwindt, M. (2014). Family Capacity-Building in Early Childhood Intervention: Do Context and Setting Matter? *School Community Journal*, 24(1), 37-48. Retrieved from https://files.eric.ed.gov/fulltext/EJ1032240.pdf

Dunst, C. J., Trivette, C. M., & Hamby, D. W. (2007). Meta-analysis of family-centered helpgiving practices research. *Mental Retardation and Developmental Disabilities Research Reviews*, 13, 370-378. doi: http://dx.doi.org/10.1002/mrdd.20176

Espe-Sherwindt, M. (2008). Family-centred practice: collaboration, competency and evidence. *Support for Learning*, 23, 136-143. doi: https://doi.org/10.1111/j.1467-9604.2008.00384.x

Ferreira, D. S. A. (2014). Qualidade de Vida Familiar e sua relação com o Suporte Social. Perceções dos cuidadores de crianças com incapacidade. Masters Dissertation in Special Education, Multi-disability domain and Cognition Problems. Escola Superior de Educação do Instituto Politécnico do Porto. Porto. Retrieved

from http://recipp.ipp.pt/bitstream/10400.22/6757/1/DM_D
ianaFerreira_2014.pdf

Fiamenghi Junior, G. A., & Messa, A. A. (2007). Pais, filhos e deficiência: estudos sobre as relações familiares. *Psicologia: Ciência e Profissão*, 27, 236-245. doi: http://dx.doi.org/10.1590/S1414-98932007000200006

Formiga, C. K., Pedrazzani, E. S., Silva, F. P. S., & Lima, C. D. (2004). Eficácia de um programa de intervenção precoce com bebês pré-termo. *Paidéia*, 14, 301-311. doi: http://dx.doi.org/10.1590/S0103-863X2004000300006

Franco, V. (2007). Dimensões transdisciplinares do trabalho de equipe em intervenção precoce. *Interação em Psicologia*, 11(1), 113-121. Retrieved from https://dspace.uevora.pt/rdpc/bitstream/10174/1331/1/ Dimens%C3%B5es%20%28publicado%29.pdf

Fundação Seade (2016). Fundação Maria Cecília Souto Vidigal. *Índice Paulista da Primeira Infância*. Retrieved from http://www.ippih.seade.gov.br/frontend/#/

Gonçalves, M. M. M. (2014). Pais, profissionais que envolvimento? Práticas centradas na família: relação técnico-família. Masters Dissertation in Education Science: Especial Education, Early Childhood Intervention Domain. Universidade Fernando Pessoa. Porto. Retrieved from https://bdigital.ufp.pt/bitstream/10284/4229/1/Mestrad o.pdf

González, A. F. Centeno, D. M., Rueda, N. M., García, J. R. O., & Peral, M. V. (2015). Calidad de vida familiar: marco de referencia, evaluación e intervención. *Ediciones Universidad de Salamanca Siglo Cero*, 46, n.254, 7-29. doi: http://dx.doi.org/10.14201/scero2015462729

Hoffman, L., Marquis, J., Poston, D., Summers, J., & Turnbull, A. (2006). Assessing Family Outcomes: Psychometric Evaluation of the Beach Center Family Quality of Life Scale. *Journal of Marriage and Family*, 68,

1069–1083. doi: https://doi.org/10.1111/j.1741-3737.2006.00314.x

Jorge, M. J., Levy, C. C. A. C., & Granato, L. (2015). Adaptação Cultural da Escala de Qualidade de Vida Familiar para o Português Brasileiro. *CoDAS*, 27, 534-540. doi: http://dx.doi.org/10.1590/2317-1782/20152014142

Macedo, E. C., Silva, R. L., Paiva, M. S., & Ramos, M. N. P. (2015). Sobrecarga e qualidade de vida de mães de crianças e adolescentes com doença crônica: revisão integrativa. *Revista Latino-Americana Enfermagem*, 23, 769-777. doi: 10.1590/0104-1169.0196.2613

Mendes, E. G. (2006). A radicalização do debate sobre a inclusão escolar no Brasil. *Revista Brasileira de Educação*, 11, 387-405. Retrieved from http://www.scielo.br/pdf/rbedu/v11n33/a02v1133.pdf

Minayo, M. C. (2008). *O desafio do conhecimento: pesquisa qualitativa em saúde*. 11ª ed. São Paulo: Hucitec.

Molinari, J. S. O., Silva, M. C. M. F., Crepaldi, M. A. (2005). Saúde e desenvolvimento da criança: A família, os fatores de risco e as ações na atenção básica. *Psicologia Argumento*, 23, 17-26. Retrieved from https://periodicos.pucpr.br/index.php/psicologiaargumento/article/view/19591/18935

Oliveira, B. H. R. (2016). PL nº 6.998 de 2013: Nas tramas de uma política pública para a primeira infância no Brasil. Dissertação de Mestrado em Ciências Sociais. Faculdade de Filosofia e Ciências Humanas, Pontifícia Universidade Católica do Rio Grande do Sul, Porto Alegre, RS, Brasil. Retrieved from http://tede2.pucrs.br/tede2/bitstream/tede/7012/2/DIS_BRUNO_HENRIQUE_RODRIGUES_DE_OLIVEIRA_COMPLETO.pdf

Pereira, A. P., & Serrano, A. M. (2014). Early Intervention in Portugal: Study of Professionals Perceptions. *Journal of*

Family Social Work, 17, 263-282. doi:10.1080/10522158.2013.865426.

Pérez, M. C. (2013). La participación de las familias en los servicios de atención temprana en la comunidad valenciana. Tesis Doctoral en Psicologia. Universidad Católica de Valencia San Vicente Mártir. Valencia. Available at https://www.educacion.gob.es/teseo/imprimirFicheroTesis. do?idFichero=pD5lUQeFIpM%3D

Peternelli, L. A. (2006). Capítulo 2: Estatística Descritiva. Retrieved from http://www.each.usp.br/rvicente/Paternelli_Cap2.pdf.

Rossetti-Ferreira, M. C. (2006). Olhando a pessoa e seus outros, de perto e de longe, no antes, aqui e depois. In Dominique Colinvaux., Luci B.Leite & Débora D. Dell'Aglio. (Org.) *Psicologia e desenvolvimento: reflexões e práticas atuais* (p.19-59). São Paulo: Casa do Psicólogo.

Sari, F. L., & Marcon, S. S. (2008). Participação da família no trabalho fisioterapêutico em crianças com paralisia cerebral. *Revista Brasileira Crescimento Desenvolvimento Humano*, 18, 229-239. Retrieved from https://www.revistas.usp.br/jhgd/article/download/198 86/21961/

Serrano, A. M. (2007). *Redes Sociais de Apoio e sua Relevância para a Intervenção Precoce*. Porto: Porto Editora.

Serrano, A. M., & Pereira, A. P. (2010). Intervenção Precoce em Portugal: Evidências e consequências. *Inclusão*, 10, 101-120. Retrieved from https://repositorium.sdum.uminho.pt/bitstream/1822/1 6154/1/Pereira%20%26%20Serrano%20%282010%29.pdf

Schalock, R. L., & Verdugo, M. A. (2002). *Calidadad de vida: Manual para profesionales de la educación, salud y servicios sociales*. Madrid: Alianza Editorial.

Educating for the equality of gender opportunities[1]

Amélia Marchão [a], Helder Henriques [a]

This text focuses on education and on the promotion of gender equality in a framework of citizenship from the kindergarten and here we present a small review of the 'state of the art' and highlight the conceptions of educators and children of pre-school age on the theme of equal gender opportunities.

We base our analysis on the results of research carried out in five kindergartens in the district of Portalegre, Portugal, using a qualitative approach, in which the participants were observed and listened to through questionnaires and interviews. The analysis developed in the course of the investigations was carried out through a process of documentary analysis, using two grids constructed for the purpose. From the intersection between the 'state of the art' and the results of the studies under analysis, it is worth noting that this issue still needs to be further addressed in kindergartens.

Introduction

At present, in the Portuguese context and in other countries as well, the need for education for the equality of gender opportunities is unquestionable. However, it is not always practised in the educational contexts of the youngest children, whether they are formal (kindergarten) or informal (family situation), despite the curricular documentation of the reference for the pre-school education mentioning it. It is about this

[1] Marchão, A. & Henriques, H. (2020). Educating for the equality of gender opportunities. In G. S. Carvalho, P. Palhares, F. Azevedo, C. Parente, C. (Coord.), *Improving children's learning and well-being* (pp. 108-128). Braga: Centro de Investigação em Estudos da Criança / Instituto de Educação. ISBN: 978-972-8952-63-1

[a] Polytechnic Institute of Portalegre, Portugal.

dichotomy, between affirmation of the need and what is effectively done in educational terms in the formal contexts of pre-school education that we will reflect throughout this text.

In this regard, it should be pointed out that the current Curricular Guidelines for Pre-school Education (OCEPE) (Silva, Marques, Mata, & Rosa, 2016), within the framework of the Content Areas established, and to be used as a reference in the organization of the curriculum, highlight the importance of education for gender equality, positioning it in Personal and Social Training, dimensions of identity and democratic coexistence and citizenship. This Content Area, considered transversal to be widely applicable aims, among other aspects, at the construction of an autonomous, fair, conscious and supportive citizenship.

OCEPE (Silva *et al.*, 2016) instructs professionals to recognize the child "as subject and agent of the educational process"[2] (p. 33) and "whose unique identity is built in social interaction, influencing and being influenced by the environment that surrounds it"[3] (p. 33), so it is necessary to be aware that the child builds her/his references through relationships and interactions with others and with the environment that welcomes and surrounds her/him. It is therefore important that these references are built in the sense of an exercise of democratic citizenship in which values such as justice, tolerance, cooperation, sharing, equality, and solidarity with others (among other values and attitudes) favour life in groups, in society in an active way, involving participation and total respect for others.

The quality of the educational environment and the values underlying the educational practice of the educator (in a close relationship with the family) constitute variables which facilitate or inhibit education for equal gender opportunities, which,

---

[2] Our translation.
[3] Our translation.

supported in the identity (being a boy, being a girl) and in the self-esteem that the child gradually builds, will guide them towards behaviours more or less "according to cultural expectations about what it is appropriate to do as a member of one or another group, expressing cultural stereotypes about men and women"[4] (Silva *et al.*, 2016, p. 34). It is up to the educator to organize and promote an educational practice that is aimed at the deconstruction of gender stereotypes, through the questioning of everyday educational situations and through a reflective approach to the attitudes, materials, resources and learning opportunities that promote and/or guides.

It is from this educational viewpoint that this text is built, unveiling the voices of the children and the voices of the educators gathered in a set of studies oriented in the scope of a Masters' degree in the area of Education, on the equality of gender opportunities and their importance in the contexts of pre-school education. Thus, the gender conceptions of children and adults are highlighted, and gender roles 'constructed' by children and adults are analysed.

Equality of gender opportunities

Vieira, Nogueira and Tavares (2012) declare that "the school, in addition to being a place of understanding and preparation for life, should be a main agent of change"[5] (p. 8) and that it has the "responsibility of becoming a privileged place of sharing, cooperation and education for participation"[6] (p. 8). These statements of the authors, in line with the general principles of the Basic Education Act of the Portuguese Educational System (Law no. 46/86), challenge the school (here understood in a broad sense and, therefore, covering the

---

[4] Our translation.
[5] Our translation.
[6] Our translation.

institutions of childhood education) to an educational action that promotes and guarantees equality of opportunities, through the training to be free citizens, responsible, autonomous and supportive through a training that appeals to the democratic and pluralistic spirit and respect for others. One of the great challenges of today's school is therefore to guarantee and promote democratic citizenship contexts in which values of freedom and justice determine egalitarian education and, therefore, teach about equal gender opportunities both in the Portuguese society and in the wider global society. As we have said before:

> There is increasing evidence of the role that the School should play in the socialization of the values of freedom, justice, plurality and equality, with the aim of ensuring that the future can bring more equitable citizenship regarding gender[7]. (Henriques & Marchão, 2016, p. 340).

Particularly in pre-school education, it is necessary to understand their contexts as a *locus* of citizenship (Vasconcelos, 2007), which is also clear from the Framework Law for Pre-school Education (Law 5/97) and of the existing OCEPE. But this is only possible when adults are guided by participatory pedagogies in which the interests and needs of the children matter and their voices are listened. The same way adults should not reproduce stereotyped speeches. Personal and Social Education, in its dimension of democratic coexistence and citizenship, will only be achieved through the promotion of educational environments that value the child, that foster the construction of his identity and that promote the construction of his critical thinking associated with values, knowledge and non-stereotyped attitudes.

---

[7] Our translation.

The Portuguese society of democratic times is unfortunately still peppered with many stereotypes that contradict equal gender opportunities, so educational action at an early age can help combat "these well-organized sets of beliefs about the characteristics of people belonging to a particular group"[8] (Cardona, Nogueira, Vieira, Uva & Tavares, 2010, p. 26). Such stereotypes usually reveal social discrimination about adults and children seen in the domestic sphere, but also in the professional sphere and in the educational sphere (Henriques & Marchão, 2016; Marchão & Henriques, 2017; Prates & Marchão, 2015).

Basow (1992) identifies stereotypes according to four categories: those relating to personality traits or attributes, those concerning roles played by women and men, those relating to professional activities and those referring to physical characteristics of men and women. In the Education, Gender and Pre-school Citizenship Guideline (Cardona *et al.*, 2010), the authors, based on research data, point out that, as a rule, the studies carried out point to a representation of the male gender characterized as stronger, more active, more competitive and more aggressive than the female gender, while the woman is represented as being better at establishing affective relationships with other people, being more caring and more capable of providing care, and being more willing to provide assistance, but still being identified as having lower self-esteem.

Several authors have contributed to supporting schools, kindergartens and their professionals in the deconstruction of gender stereotypes (among them, Castro & Barbosa, 2000; Rodrigues, 2003; Neto *et al.*, 2000; Cardona *et al.*, 2010, Vieira, Nogueira & Tavares, 2012), and the Commission for Citizenship and Gender Equality (CIG) has done a great deal of work through the promotion, support and financing of training for childhood

---

[8] Our translation.

educators and teachers. This has been particularly through the publication of Education, Gender and Citizenship Guidelines for Pre-school Education and for other levels of Basic and Secondary Education, which are available in paper format and through free online access on their website (https://www.cig.gov.pt/).

The *Cadernos Coeducación*[9] collection has been another important contribution of the CIG. In this collection important contributions have been made enabling kindergartens and schools to help, through their educational practices, to deconstruct stereotypes, which naturally leads to the creation of environments conducive to the construction of the child's identity and self-esteem in relationship with the values of democratic life. "The construction of identity involves the recognition of individual characteristics and the understanding of each individual's abilities and difficulties, whatever they may be"[10] (Silva *et al.*, 2016, p. 34) and gender identity, which is a "social label by which two groups of people are distinguished"[11] (Rodrigues, 2003, p. 17)' begins to emerge in the child between two and five years old, as the child appropriates the notion of gender and demonstrates it in his or her daily routine through behaviours and attitudes, often developed in situations of play. At that age the child responds socially according to the models that pervade in his or her surroundings, femininity or masculinity, reproducing them and learning the role of the feminine and the masculine from those who are close to her/him, although, as Martin (1989) says, cited by Cardona *et al* (2010), it is only around eight to nine years of age that most children are able to understand more clearly the issues and expectations associated with gender. However, these roles can be very stereotyped according to the different types of

---

[9] Cadernos Coeducação.
[10] Our translation.
[11] Our translation.

stereotypes identified by Basow (1992), both in attitudes and behaviour and in play situations.

Deconstructing gender stereotypes in kindergarten is not an easy task and requires the assumption of coeducational practices that foster respect and cooperation between boys and girls and enable them to construct an egalitarian view and attitude to gender respect, based on a citizenship that implies "an individual and collective commitment to the rights and duties that we all face before others"[12] (Henriques & Marchão, 2016, p. 343).

As Monge, Rosário and Cañamero (2000) say, the deconstruction of stereotypes must begin with reflection on and discussion of the school curriculum and the awareness that "the transmission of informal messages among social actors structures the daily interactions which reproduce the sexist stereotypes and prejudices"[13] (p.12). Adults in an educational/school context are not always aware of their conceptions and stereotypes and the fact that in interactions and in daily life they are themselves transmitters of the existing gender discrimination in society, instead of assuming, as facilitators of an educational culture centred on plurality, tolerance for different options and a critical awareness of the influence that their own attitudes and behaviours have in the formation of a child with an egalitarian vision in relation to gender opportunity.

Thus, it is argued, there is a need for an educational intervention that values gender equality from the earliest years and addresses the need to produce more knowledge in this area. This field of research is not being adequately explored, and in Portugal there are not many studies *focusing* on early childhood education associated with gender equality education at the pre-school age, although there have been academic studies (some of which we have already mentioned), as is the case of the studies

---

[12] Our translation.
[13] Our translation.

we conducted (Bento, 2011; Duarte, 2013; Prates, 2014; Alvanel, 2015; Cabral, 2015), and which served as the fundamental theme for the collective interpretation that is shared in this text . It should be noted, however, that other levels of teaching and/or teaching resources (such as textbooks) aimed at older children/young people have been studied more frequently by different authors.

Methodological script

The framework of analysis and reflection presented in this text is based on research conducted in the framework of two Masters' degrees in education (pre-school education and education and protection of children and young people and those at-risk) carried out in a polytechnic institution. Two analytical grids (A - adult answers; B - children's answers) were used for this purpose, and these were applied after similar objectives had been verified in the studies under analysis (Bento, 2011; Duarte, 2013; Prates, 2014; Alvanel, 2015; Cabral, 2015) namely to establish gender roles of children and adults and in that way to use the survey as one of the main data collection instruments.

The grids have yes or no as possible answers, illustrations from the studies and comments from the authors of the present text. Grid A was made by items referring to: adult gender conception; importance given to the education for gender equality; and activities developed in the gender equality education. Grid B was made by items referring to: gender conceptions - gender identity; role gender; and decisions on toys, activities and colours.

These research-action studies (four studies - Bento, 2011; Duarte, 2013; Alvanel, 2015; Cabral, 2015) and the case study (one study - Prates, 2014) had as context five kindergarten (one per study) from Portalegre district, Portugal, and used a qualitative approach, involving the participants being observed and their views heard through questionnaires (adult questionnaires and interviews with adults and children).

The questionnaires were applied to a total of nine educators, each with more than ten years of professional experience, and included open and closed answers. The interviews were applied to eight educators with more than ten years of professional experience and included dimensions as: gender conceptions; importance given to the education for gender equality; activities developed in the gender equality education.

The interviews made to children had as starting point the deconstruction of small narratives and aim to check, among others: gender conceptions - gender identity; gender roles given to masculine and to feminine; gender conception associated with stereotypes on playing and toys, colours and professions. These interviews were applied to 97 children with five and six years old, in average 19.4 children per kindergarten. The small narratives are short texts in which small problems are given to children for them to solve.

In the process of document analysis that we carried out through the grids, the main objective was: (i) to understand the gender conceptions of children and adults; and (ii) to identify the importance that adults attribute to education for gender equality and how they mobilize it in pedagogical practice. The grid (A) was applied, entering the responses given by the adults interviewed and expressed in the reports of each one of the studies. These entries were then compared with the interpretation of the authors of the studies, resulting in the combination of all the answers brought together and subject to the collective analysis and interpretation presented in this text. In the case of interviews conducted with the children, the process of applying the analysis grid (B) was similar, the only change being an additional analysis item referring to the narratives used as the starting point of the interviews.

To support the analysis and interpretation developed, beyond the state of the art, it has contributed the experience of the authors of this text in continuous training actions with childhood educators. This continuous training had the objective of promoting and sharing educational experiences on education for equal gender opportunities (Marchão & Henriques, 2017).

Children and adults' conceptions: gender and gender roles

We begin by presenting and interpreting the gender conceptions identified from the questionnaire responses and interviews carried out with the responsible adults – a total of 17 childhood educators.

Most educators assume that they are not sufficiently trained/informed on gender equality issues in pre-school education. Generally, in the five studies, there is some confusion among the educators between the term "gender" and the term "sex". This confusion between the two terms is not exclusive to the participants of these studies, and the terms are often used synonymously. However, as we know, the term sex "is used to distinguish individuals on the basis of their belonging to one of the biological categories"[14] (Cardona *et al.*, 2010, p. 12), assuming the differentiation of individuals through characteristics fundamentally biological, and the term gender refers to the set of cultural and social expectations associated with masculine or feminine individuals. Gender is, therefore, a sociocultural category "used to describe inferences and meanings attributed to individuals from the knowledge of their sexual category of belonging"[15] (Cardona *et al.*, 2010, p. 12). This category is much broader than the category of sex and includes identity aspects stemming from society and culture, "anchoring themselves in

---

[14] Our translation.
[15] Our translation.

psychological attributes and cultural appropriations"[16] (Henriques & Marchão, 2014), which vary in space and time.

Thirteen educators out of the total of 17 present gender concepts that we can classify as based on stereotypes that do not conform to a democratic society in which principles of equal opportunities of gender are in force. As an example, it is said that for the majority, it is natural to associate the profession of childhood educator with the feminine since they represent it as a profession associated with a certain maternal condition (Prates, 2014; Alvanel, 2105; Cabral, 2015). Although the professions of childhood in the Portuguese context involve more women than men it does not seem natural to us in the twenty-first century that some of the participants in these studies assume that their profession is identified more with the feminine and to find that there is no research that supports such an association which can therefore only be based on a stereotyped reproduction of gender roles associated with professions. As Cardona *et al* (2010) say, based on ideas that do not have scientific support:

> The family and all other socializing agents continue to educate the boy and the girl differently for the performance of the most varied roles throughout life, as if biological differentiation determined personal characteristics, development opportunities and pathways[17] (Cardona, *et al.*, 2010, p. 17).

It is therefore important that the education of younger children "is no longer regarded as a predominantly feminine task"[18] (Cardona *et al.*, 2010, p. 60).

Another aspect resulting from the collection of educators' opinions has to do with some lack of awareness in the use of gender stereotypes in the context and daily life of the

---

[16] Our translation.

[17] Our translation.

[18] Our translation.

118

kindergarten (this aspect was also confirmed through observations made in the conducted studies although not presented in this text). Although saying they are adults who advocate equal opportunities for men and women most educators do not give examples of activities and strategies that they use specifically for this, only referring to the fact that they use children's attitudes or behaviours in the pedagogical everyday life in order to make them reflect and think about gender equality. This use seems fundamental in the context of a pedagogy that places the child and her/his ideas at the centre; however, we must emphasize the need for learning opportunities in favour of a Personal and Social Training that is consistent with active citizenship, specifically respect for others, fairness and support. With this aim the organization of the educational environment must also be considered, in particular the locations and the organization of the groups, as well as the pedagogical resources. The educator's behaviour and the way she organizes the educational environment is crucial for children to discuss the gender questions in a democratic way (Cardona, *et al.*, 2010).

Research, continuous training and the resources available for gender equality education (some of which we have already mentioned and are from the CIG) are essential so the adults responsible for children become aware of the need to include appropriate educational actions in this education for citizenship, since to educate for citizenship is to educate for equal opportunities of gender.

However, most of the educators questioned and interviewed revealed that they did not have much knowledge of materials and resources that could be used in pedagogical routine and gave verbal interaction as one of the main strategies that they use to deconstruct stereotypes that children present in situations, behaviours and attitudes emerging in everyday life. In the scope of Personal Training of the Child and the education for citizenship this interaction is of great importance, but educators need to go further. The Gender and Pre-school Citizenship Education Guide (Cardona, *et al.* 2010) is an excellent contribution in this regard and can be a reference resource in the practice of educators. The Guide establishes some recommendations about the organization of the educational environment, about the organization of the group, and about the role that the professional should have, and it also exemplifies some activities that can, as appropriate for each group of children, be taken as examples and also used for (self) evaluation, whether such evaluation refers to the educational process or the children's learning. In particular, regarding activities, the Guide proposes discussion groups in which all children participate, brainstorming, role-playing, and case studies, supported by strategies like the photo word or the technique of testimony.

We now present the conceptions of children ascertained through the interviews (and confirmed in sessions of observations used in the development of the studies under analysis, which are not explored in this text), and also comment on how to interpret them.

From the deconstruction of a narrative created by each of the authors of the studies under analysis, the set of 97 children presented concepts associated with gender identity and gender roles which we added to a set of categories, as evidenced by the authors (Bento, 2011; Duarte, 2013; Prates, 2014; Alvanel, 2015; Cabral, 2015). These categories refer to the concepts on gender, gender roles, children's decisions about toys and/or activities and colours considered appropriate for a boy or girl.

For the conceptions about gender, it was found that all children assumed and expressed a certain notion of gender through the term boy or girl. Their conceptions related to aspects of their physique, but also appearance (hair length, for example), reference to sex in a physiological dimension, and the aspects of their own games (Gispert, 1999), with some stereotypes being identified. Children, like adults, but more naturally given their age, find it difficult to distinguish between the term sex and the term gender, constructing their ideas according to the specificities of their physique or appearance. However, as we have already mentioned, the term:

> Gender cannot mean the same as sex, (...) as sex refers to the biological identity of a person, while gender is linked to its social construction as male or female, and in this construction is implicit the idea of relationship[19] (Rodrigues, 2003, p. 17).

The same author (2003) states that "as gender becomes stable, children learn gender stereotypes by observing the actions and gender roles of men and women surrounding them"[20] (p. 24) and show them in their own games, where many gender roles can be observed.

Concerning the assumption of gender roles, through the interviews it was possible to identify that the children identify roles that men and women assume according to their family and/or educational environment. That is, they identify gender roles and functions through the behaviours and attitudes of the mother or the father and the educator, with the majority associating the mother with domestic and caring tasks and the father with working outside the home and resting in the domestic context. In a typical application of these roles, the mother is the one who does the most cooking, washing the dishes, and sweeping the floor, for example, and the father is "always" sitting on the sofa, and does not vacuum the house or wash dishes. However, a third of the children already say that the father helps the mother, for example in making dinner, shopping, or taking the children to school.

---

[19] Our translation.
[20] Our translation.

Still in this scope of gender roles, most children identify professions for men (fireman, policeman, doctor, engineer) and for women (teacher, educator, nurse, housekeeper) according to their domestic sphere and according to the social interactions they have established in their daily lives.

From an analysis of their responses, one discerns gender stereotypes related to physical characteristics, with gender roles relating to professional activities that need to be deconstructed. As Rodrigues (2003, p. 18) points out: "the acquisition by the child of normal gender roles is a fundamental aspect of the development and adjustment of the whole personality"[21].

This attitude and stereotyped thinking persist regarding another identified conception that associated with toys, games, and the colour of clothes, these being choices associated with masculine and feminine by most children. The boys choose toys and games with which they identify most, related to sport (soccer), danger and heroes associated with fighting games and strength, and girls choose dolls, princesses and other aesthetic accessories (earrings, bracelets) and toys socially associated with the feminine. The colour of the clothing is one of the strong elements in the association with the feminine and the masculine, pink being more associated with the feminine universe, which also admits as normal the use of all the colours, including the blue one for both genders.

Cardona *et al* (2010) based on research by Ruble and Martin (1998), point out that:

> Children between 3 and 6 years of age tend to make more stereotyped descriptions of themselves and others than adults. They believe [Ruble & Martin,

---

[21] Our translation.

1998], however, that stereotypes apply more to boys and girls of their age than to older people[22] (p. 31).

Summarizing, it is necessary to bet in a training and educational dynamic for adults and children. It is needed to consider that citizenship is "a state in which the person (or the citizen) has the rights and / or obligations associated with belonging to an extended community, especially the state"[23] (Cardona, *et al.*, 2010, p. 33). In the education for citizenship gender questions are included and it is important to work them with the younger children.

Final considerations

The overall formation of the child, as a person, requires the adoption of educational practices that emphasize, among other objectives, those that refer to personal and social formation and to the construction of the person as an emancipated citizen along with values and dispositions such as justice, respect, equality, and solidarity with others, among other values. The earlier a child is provided with an environment of democratic coexistence and citizenship, the more easily he/she appropriates democratic values and a sense of fairness.

Consequently, it is important that pedagogical practices based on participation be implemented in childhood education, and that the child should be raised to a central status, allowing the child to construct his/her identity, self-esteem, independence and autonomy far from stereotypes that deny the possibility of equal opportunities for gender.

Such practices are not easy to implement since it is often a question of mediating interactions among people, while being an example, since the values of democracy are not taught, they are

---

[22] Our translation.
[23] Our translation.

practised. As it has been shown throughout this text, adults are not always aware of their own stereotyped attitudes, opinions and actions, nor are they adequately equipped with knowledge and educational resources appropriate to practices free of stereotypes. It is therefore necessary to introduce in the initial and continuing training of educators a dimension of training/education for citizenship, whether from the point of view of general educational training or training in teaching.

Also the children listened to in the research studies analysed showed that in the construction of their identity, as is expected and verified through the investigation, their gender identity is already visible assuming masculine and feminine in a way associated with patterns and roles that they observe in the adult people who surround them. The concepts and opinions they express are not free from stereotypes, as is verified in their games, in their actions and in their voices; that is, the stereotypes observed refer to the categories referred to by Basow (1992), namely: those referring to personality traits and attributes, those referring to the roles played by men and women, those related to the professions and those concerning the physical characteristics of men and women.

The child's path in kindergarten and at school must provide him/her with skills that allow him/her to begin to exercise citizenship centred on values of equity between men and women and, therefore, assume the importance of education for the gender equality as an essential condition in the formation of the younger child-person. The plasticity of the child's cognitive abilities, still in the process of being structured and maturating, allows them to alter their conceptions in accordance with the positive examples and interactions that they are experiencing. The deconstruction of gender stereotypes is a work of the kindergarten along with the family and should be guided by a solid educational goal, based on personal and social development and in which the feminine and the masculine are promoted with equal opportunities.

References

Alvanel, A. (2015). *O Jogo Simbólico e a Construção da Identidade de Género.* (Relatório do Mestrado em Educação Pré-escolar). Portalegre: Escola Superior de Educação do Instituto Politécnico de Portalegre. Obtido de http://hdl.handle.net/10400.26/9180

Basow, S. (1992). *Gender stereotypes and roles.* Pacific Grove, Brooks/Cole.

Bento, A. (2011). *Promoção da igualdade de género em contexto de educação pré-escolar.* (Relatório do Mestrado em Educação Pré-escolar). Potalegre: Escola Superior de Educação do Instituto Politécnico de Portalegre. Obtido de http://hdl.handle.net/10400.26/2146

Cabral, V. (2015). *Educar para a Cidadania Através de Práticas de Igualdade de Género na Educação Pré-escolar.* (Relatório do Mestrado em Educação Pré-escolar). Portalegre: Escola Superior de Educação do Instituto Politécnico de Portalegre. Obtido de http://hdl.handle.net/10400.26/14269

Cardona, M. J. (Coord.), Nogueira, C., Uva, M., & Tavares, T. C. (2010). *Guião de Educação, Género e Cidadania Pré-escolar.* Lisboa: Comissão para a Cidadania e Igualdade de Género.

Castro, I., Barbosa, F., & (Orgs). (2000). *Coeducar para uma sociedade inclusiva.* Lisboa: Comissão para a Igualdade e para os Direitos das Mulheres. Presidência do Conselho de Ministros.

Duarte, J. (2013). *Promoção da Igualdade de Género na Educação Pré-escolar Através do Guião de Educação, Género e Cidadania.* (Relatório do Mestrado em Educação Pré-escolar). Portalegre: Escola Superior de Educação do Instituto Politécnico de Portalegre. Obtido de http://hdl.handle.net/10400.26/5092

Gispert, C. (1999). *Enciclopédia de Psicologia*. Lisboa: Liarte.

Henriques, H., & Marchão, A. (2014). Género, cidadania e práticas educativas: a promoção da igualdade em contextos educativos. Em SPCE, *Actas do XII Congresso da Sociedade Portuguesa de Ciências da Educação* (pp. 1855-1863). Vila Real: Universidade de Trás-os Montes, UTAD.

Henriques, H., & Marchão, A. (2016). Educação para a igualdade de género: leituras a partir da realidade de cinco jardins de infância do distrito de Portalegre, Portugal. *Foro de Educación, 14(20),* 339-360. *doi: http://dx.doi.org/10.14516/fde.2016.014.020.017*

Henriques, H., & Marchão, A. (2017). Educar para a cidadania em educação pré-escolar: OCEPE, guiões e curricula. In V. M. Pires, *II Encontro Internacional de Formação na Docência (INCTE): Livro de atas* (pp. 689-696). Bragança: Instituto Politécnico de Bragança. Obtido de http://hdl.handle.net/10198/4960

Marchão, A., & Henriques, H. (2015). Educação, Cidadania e Igualdade de Oportunidades: olhares sobre a educação de infância. *Revista Aprender, n.º 36 acedido em http://www.esep.pt/aprender/index.php/revistas/116-revista-aprender-n-36*, pp. 72-85.

Marchão, A., & Henriques, H. (2017). Igualdade de género: uma reflexão crítica a partir do jardim de infância. In M. V. Pires, *II Encontro Internacional de Formação na Docência (INCTE): Livro de atas* (pp. 697-704). Bragança: Instituto Politécnico de Bragança. Obtido de http://hdl.handle.net/10198/4960

Neto, A., Cid, M., Pomar, C., Peças, A., Chaleta, E., Folque, A., & Martins, A. (2000). *Estereótipos de género*. Lisboa: Comissão para a Cidadania e Igualdade de Género.

Monge, M. G., Rosário, M., & Cañamero, G. (2000). *Criatividade na coeduação. Uma estratégia para a mudança*. Lisboa: Comissão para a Igualdade e para os Direitos das Mulheres.

Prates, M. (2014). *Educação para a igualdade de género: um estudo de caso numa instituição de educação de infância.* (Dissertação de Mestrado em Educação e Proteção de Crianças e Jovens em Risco). Portalegre: Escola Superior de Educação do Instituto Politécnico de Portalegre. Obtido de http://hdl.handle.net/10400.26/6134

Prates, M., & Marchão, A. (2015). Estudo das conceções de género presentes num jardim-de-infância da cidade da Ponte de Sor: as conceções das crianças, das educadoras e dos/as encarregados/as de educação. *Revista Aprender*, 86-101. Obtido de http://legado.esep.pt/aprender/index.php/revistas/116-revista-aprender-n-36

Rodrigues, P. (2003). *Questões de género na infância: marcas de identidade.* Lisboa: Instituto Piaget.

Silva, I. (Coord.), Marques, L., Mata, L., & Rosa, M. (2016). *Orientações curriculares para a Educação Pré-escolar.* Lisboa: Ministério da Educação/Direção-Geral da Educação (DGE).

Vasconcelos, T. (2007). A importância da educação na construção da cidadania. *Saber (e) Educar, n.º 12*, 109-117.

Vieira, C., Nogueira, C., & Tavares, T. (2012). Género e cidadania. Em C. Pomar, (Coord.), A. Balsa, A. Conde, A. García, A. García, T. Tavares, *Guião de Educação, Género e Cidadania. 2.º Ciclo* (pp. 7-48). Lisboa: Comissão para Cidadania e Igualdade de Género.

Legal documents

Basic Education Act of the Portuguese Educational System (Law no. 46/86), Law no. 46/86 published in the Diário da Republica on October 14, 1st Series, number 237/1986.

Framework Law on Pre-school Education, Law no. 5/97 published in the Diário da República on February 10, Series I-A, nº. 34/1997.

The english translation was the responsibility of Vanda Grácio Ribeiro, professor in the Polytechnic Institute of Portalegre, vribeiro@ipportalegre.pt

Doctoral Degree in Child Studies

The cycle of studies leading to the doctoral degree in *Child Studies* has the duration of 3 years (full-time schedule), which corresponds to 180 ECTS, and is organized in five specialities:
- Artistic Education
- Childhood, Culture and Society
- Childhood, Development and Learning
- Physical Education and Child Health
- Special Education

This cycle of studies is primarily aimed at the development of: systematic understanding capabilities in a scientific field of study; research competencies, skills and methods associated with a scientific field; the ability to conceive, design, adapt and perform significant research, respecting the requirements imposed by the academic standards for quality and integrity.

This cycle of studies includes: one curricular component that combines course units common to the various doctoral specialities, each possessing specific course units, and with transversal course units; the development of an original and especially designed thesis for this purpose, appropriate to the knowledge branch and doctoral speciality.
The conclusion of this Doctoral degree allows the realization of research activity at post-doctoral level.

Contatcts
Universidade do Minho
Instituto de Educação
Campus de Gualtar
4710-057 Braga | Portugal
Tel.: +351253604240 Fax: +351253604659
E-Mail: sec-dout-ec@ie.uminho.pt; sec@ie.uminho.pt
URL: https://www.ie.uminho.pt